DSCA HANDBOOK

FOR

FOREIGN ASSISTANCE ACT (FAA)

DRAWDOWN OF DEFENSE ARTICLES AND SERVICES

PREFACE

Drawdowns are different from normal Security Assistance procedures, and very important tools for furthering U.S. foreign policy objectives. Key players in the drawdown process are the Country Program/Financial Directors, as well as other personnel within DSCA.

A drawdown is one of the very unique times when the Commander-in-Chief, placing full trust and confidence in you, empowers you to effect a change in international relations. Although the drawdown of Department of Defense articles, services and training is generally coordinated through existing Security Assistance channels using the basic policies and guidelines already in-place, usually, time is of the essence. Drawdowns do not occur that often and as a result we fully recognize that you need help in wading through this sometimes-mysterious world.

This handbook is a guide for you and other Defense Security Cooperation Agency (DSCA) personnel who become involved in the planning and execution of drawdowns. It is not intended to serve as a regulation, and consequently should not be construed as one. That said, this guide builds upon two earlier editions and contains the wisdom of some of the best and brightest professionals in the Security Cooperation Community.

Keith B. Webster
Director
Business Operations/Comptroller
DSCA

Freda J. Lodge
Director
Policy, Plans and Programs
DSCA

TABLE OF CONTENTS

Page

TABLE OF CONTENTS, Continued

TABLE OF CONTENTS, Continued

TABLE OF CONTENTS, Continued

TABLES

Table	Title	

TABLE OF CONTENTS, Continued

REFERENCES

DoD 5105.38-M, "Security Assistance Management Manual," October 3, 2003

DoD 7000.14-R, Department of Defense Financial Management Regulations (FMRS), Volume 11b, Chapter 55, October 2002. Volume 12, Chapter 23, Section 2305

U.S. Army Regulation 725-50 (AR 725-50)

C1. CHAPTER 1

PURPOSE

C1.1. THE PURPOSE OF DRAWDOWNS

Drawdowns allow the President of the United States to respond to unforeseen emergencies and other requirements without having to first seek additional legislative authority or budgetary appropriations. These include peacekeeping operations, narcotics control, international disaster assistance, antiterrorism assistance, nonproliferation assistance, migration and refugee assistance, and prisoner of war/missing in action (POW/MIA) efforts in Cambodia, Laos, and Vietnam. From a legal perspective, a drawdown is the execution of statutory authority that permits the disposition of United States property or services. On an exceptional basis, specific legislation may authorize the procurement of articles and services provided by drawdown.

C1.2. THE PURPOSE OF THIS HANDBOOK

C1.2.1. This handbook is a general guide for action-level personnel in planning and executing drawdowns of DoD defense articles in stock and defense services. There is no one directive that governs Presidential Determinations (PD). However, the following DoD regulations and manuals should be used in addition to this handbook:

C1.2.1.1. DoD 4141-R, Materiel Management Regulation, Chapter 4. --Asset Management

C1.2.1.2. DoD 5105.38-M, October 3, 2003, Security Assistance Management Manual (SAMM), Chapters 2, 8, 10, 11, 13, and Appendix 5 (searchable electronic version can be located at http://www.dsca.mil/samm).

C1.2.1.3. DoD Financial Management Regulation (DoDFMR) 7000.14R, Volume 15, Chapter 7 (Pricing). The electronic version can be found at URL: http://www.dtic.mil/comptroller/fmr

C1.2.2. The drawdown of DoD articles and services is generally coordinated and executed through existing Security Assistance channels using the basic policies and guidelines already in place. Each Action Officer should therefore refer to appropriate legislation, policy guidance, and procedures already in existence in planning and executing drawdowns. However, the basic steps in a drawdown are the same and are identified in subsequent chapters.

C1.2.3. This handbook highlights those elements of drawdown actions that differ from regular Security Assistance procedures.

C1.2.4. The most critical element in understanding drawdowns is that there is normally NO budget authority (no funding) associated with drawdowns. U.S. Government (USG) agencies providing articles and services under drawdowns must absorb the impact associated with the drawdowns within their budgets. Except for transportation and related services where new contracts would cost less than providing such services with DoD assets, no new procurement is authorized and no new money may be placed on existing contracts. As a matter of law, only articles and services already in DoD stocks may be drawn down. Recent exceptions to this rule occurred in the case of drawdowns for Afghanistan [Afghanistan Freedom Support Act (AFSA) P.L. 107-327] and Iraq [Iraq Liberation Act of 1998 (P.L. 105-338) (the "Act")], where drawdown of funds was authorized by law.

C1.2.5. A basic premise to keep in mind is that there are NO standard drawdowns. All drawdowns will vary with degree of urgency, political pressure, time-lines, and degree to which the Services can support the proposed drawdown without adverse operational or financial impact.

CHAPTER 1

C2. CHAPTER 2

OVERVIEW OF DRAWDOWN TYPES

C2.1. DEFINITION

For lack of any official terminology, drawdowns can best be characterized as Emergency or Non-Emergency drawdowns.

C2.2. EMERGENCY DRAWDOWNS

The traditional drawdown is normally precipitated by an emergency in a foreign country or region. An example was the devastation caused by hurricane Mitch in the Americas a number of years ago.

C2.2.1. In emergency drawdowns, the Department of Defense (DoD), U. S. Department of State (DoS), and National Security Council (NSC) coordinate the United States Government (USG) response with implementing agencies and organizations. This ad hoc interagency process determines which existing statutory authority applies to the situation and identifies which articles and services should be provided.

C2.2.2. Potential contributing executive agencies (e.g. Department of Defense, U.S. Department of the Treasury (DoT), U. S. Department of Justice (DoJ)) and the Military Services furnish Valuation and Availability (V&A) data indicating the estimated value of the articles and services proposed for the drawdown. The V&As are retained by the Military Services furnishing the data and the DSCA Country Program Director (CPD) maintains copies of the data for the applicable drawdown.

C2.2.3. The resulting estimate of articles/services and the scope of support forms the basis for the subsequent Presidential Determination (PD) authorizing a specific dollar value for the drawdown authority, which may be executed in the situation.

C2.2.4. The time-line for starting execution of emergency drawdowns may be as short as 24-48 hours, but more commonly takes 1-2 weeks.

C2.3. NON-EMERGENCY DRAWDOWNS

Drawdowns may be authorized in non-emergency situations to support mid- to long-term foreign policy initiatives, rather than to respond to emergencies. The procedure for starting and executing a non-emergency drawdown is similar to the procedure for an emergency drawdown, with the following variations.

C2.3.1. In non-emergency situations, the value of the drawdown is set forth in existing or special legislative authority and further stated in the PD. As requirements are refined, a major focus of some of these drawdown efforts has been to "use up the authority" (i.e., execute the full value of the PD).

C2.3.2. The time-line to determine requirements for such drawdowns is often extended from one to six months before an Execute Order (EXORD) is issued. The EXORD is the operational requirement document for the Services. Delivery of articles and services may take an extended period of time. Articles and services to be provided tend to be more long-term oriented, e.g. allocation and refurbishment of end items.

C2.3.3. Such drawdowns "end" when the termination date established in the EXORD is reached. Accordingly, there is likely to be a mid-course financial reconciliation of "actual" versus "projected" costs. If the value of the PD has not yet been exhausted, new items may be potentially added to the drawdown via a new EXORD.

C2.3.4. <u>Drawdowns -- Recent Trends</u>. In recent years, the drawdown of DoD articles and services has increased. From 1980 to 1992, 25 drawdowns were executed for an aggregate PD value of $652.02 M. Between 1993 and May 2004, there were 61 drawdowns with total PD value of $2.3B. Recent drawdowns have been used to build up the recipient's long-term military capability (Bosnia, Jordan, Mexico, Colombia, etc.) as well as to respond to emergent military (e.g., Sierra Leone) or humanitarian (e.g., Venezuela, Southern Africa) crises. A list of DoD drawdowns and the record values began in 1963 and has continued through May 2004. Appendix 1 provides a complete list of these drawdowns and their values.

C3. CHAPTER 3

STATUTORY AUTHORITY

C3.1. GENERAL

Drawdowns are authorized either under the Foreign Assistance Act of 1961 as amended (FAA), or under special legislative provisions.

C3.2. STANDING DRAWDOWN AUTHORITIES

Statutes in force for the drawdowns of USG articles and services are listed in Table C3.T1 below. This replicates the information that may be found in table C11.T5 of the Security Assistance Management Manual (SAMM).

C3.2.1. Table C3.T1 summarizes the drawdown authorities and their differences.

Table C3.T1. Drawdown Legislation Summary (Table C11.T5 of the SAMM)

Legislation	Subject
FAA, Section 506(a)(1) [22 U.S.C. 2318(a)(1)] (reference (b) SAMM)	DoD Drawdown for unforeseen emergencies: – Authorizes the President to direct DoD drawdowns for unforeseen emergencies requiring immediate military assistance that cannot be addressed under the AECA or any other law. – Only defense articles already on hand in DoD stocks, DoD services, and military education and training may be provided. – Congress must be notified before the President signs the Presidential Determination (PD). – The aggregate value of all drawdowns directed in any fiscal year under FAA, section 506(a)(1) (reference (b)) may not exceed $100M.

FAA, Section 506(a)(2) [22 U.S.C. 2318(a)(2)] (reference (b) SAMM)	International narcotics control, international disaster assistance, antiterrorism assistance, nonproliferation assistance, migration and refugee assistance, Prisoner of War/Missing in Action (POW/MIA) efforts in Cambodia, Laos and Vietnam:
	– Inventory and resources of any USG agency may be provided.
	– Congress must be notified before the President signs the PD for international disaster relief and POW/MIA efforts in Vietnam, Cambodia, and Laos.
	– Congress must be notified 15 days before the President signs the PD for international narcotics control and efforts under the Migration and Refugee Assistance Act of 1962.
	– The aggregate value of all drawdowns directed in any fiscal year under FAA, section 506(a)(2) (reference (b)) may not exceed $200M of which:
	  – No more than $75M may come from the Department of Defense.
	  – No more than $75M may be used for international narcotics control.
	  – No more than $15M may be used for POW/MIA drawdowns.

Legislation	Subject
FAA, Section 552(c)(2) [22 U.S.C. 2348a(c)(2)] (reference (b) SAMM)	Peacekeeping Operations: – Authorizes drawdown if the President determines that an unforeseen emergency requires the immediate provision of commodities and services of any USG agency to countries and international organizations to support peacekeeping operations. – Congress must be notified before the President signs the PD. – The aggregate value of drawdowns directed under FAA, section 552(c)(2) (reference (b)) may not exceed $25M per fiscal year. United Nations support may be limited to $3 million per fiscal year per operation; Public Law 106-113, section 724 (22 U.S.C. 287b and 287c(2)) (reference (ck)).
FAA, Section 503 (reference (b) SAMM)	General authority to furnish Military Assistance under the FAA.
FAA, Section 505 (reference (b) SAMM)	Conditions of eligibility for Military Assistance under the FAA.
FAA, Section 652 [22 U.S.C. 2411] (reference (b) SAMM)	Congressional Notification required before the President can direct drawdowns or exercise other specified special authorities under the FAA.
Public Law No. 106-113 [22 U.S.C. 287b] [22 U.S.C. 287e(2)] (reference (ck) SAMM)	Support to the United Nations.
Special Legislative Authorities	Congress may create special legislation for specific programs or purposes. There is no annual limit on the amount of special authorities that Congress may authorize. Special authorities give the President the legislative authority to provide assistance, but it is a Presidential decision whether to use that authority. Legislation for special authorities may provide for broader drawdown assistance, including authorization to contract for articles, services, and education and training that are NOT on hand.
Cargo Preference Act of 1954 (reference (bd) SAMM)	All drawdowns items transferred by ocean carriers must follow U.S. cargo preference requirements. Recipient countries must use U.S. flag vessels unless the Maritime Administration (MARAD) has issued a non-availability waiver. MARAD assists in monitoring these statutes. The MILDEPs must consider cargo preference requirements when considering transportations options for drawdowns. The responsible office at MARAD is: U.S. Department of Transportation Maritime Administration Office of Cargo Preference 400 Seventh St. SW Washington, DC 20590

C3.3. SIGNIFICANT ADDITIONAL LEGISLATIVE AUTHORITIES THAT RELATE TO DRAWDOWNS

C3.3.1. Enhanced End Use Monitoring (EUM). Enhanced EUM is required for sensitive defense articles, services, and technologies; defense articles provided under the provision of FAA, section 505; and technology transfers made within sensitive political situations. For sensitive articles and/or services, EXORDs may contain specialized notes requiring greater physical security and accountability contingent on the principal of trust with verification. In addition to routine observations, EUM of these items may require a compliance visit to the host government by a Defense Security Cooperation Agency (DSCA)-led team.

C4. CHAPTER 4

GOVERNING POLICY AND PROCEDURES

C4.1. POLICY DOCUMENTATION

There is no single document that provides all policy guidance and procedures for drawdowns. Unless otherwise noted, normal Security Assistance procedures apply.

C4.2. POLICIES AND GUIDELINES

As we have executed drawdowns in recent years, the following unique drawdown policies and guidelines have evolved:

C4.2.1. Equipment to be provided must be physically on hand (excess or non-excess).

C4.2.2. Except for transportation, no new contracts (including placing orders against existing contracts) are authorized. Equipment, spares, and other items must already be in DoD stocks. Supplies or services under existing DoD contracts may be used for drawdown purposes if the use is within the scope of the PD, and funds have been previously obligated. Inventory Control Points (ICPs) must process requisitions with "Fill or Kill" advice codes (2J, 31, 32, etc. as appropriate). On an exceptional basis, legislation authorizes the procurement of articles and services provided by drawdown. New contracts for transportation and related services may be incurred for a drawdown if the cost to acquire such transportation and services is less than the cost to use DoD assets

C4.2.3. The Services must reimburse Defense Working Capital Funds (DWCFs) for all materiel and services provided. These costs should be accounted for under the current year operations and maintenance (O&M) budget. Refer to FMR Volume 12, Chapter 23, Section 2305. Memo at Appendix 2 has been incorporated and cited as a reference in Volume 12, Chapter 23, Section 2302 for the policy from the Office of the Secretary of Defense (Comptroller). (Examples of DWCF can be found at: http://www.dod.mil/comptroller/icenter/dwcf/dhintro.htm.

C4.2.4. Fuel drawdowns are handled in the same way as DWCF materials. The Defense Energy Support Center (DESC) under Defense Logistics Agency (DLA) manages fuel contracts for all the Services. As a rule, the Services do not hold large inventories of fuel. DESC's bulk fuel contracts allow the Services to procure fuel on an "as-needed," "just-in-time" basis. As with any other commodity, the Services can utilize O&M or Working Capital Fund (WCF) obligational authority to fund, via Military Inter-departmental Purchase Request (DD Form 448, MIPR), fuel drawdowns supplied from DESC existing contracts. Use of this funding can impact obligational authority for normal Services operations; therefore such issues should be carefully coordinated with the Services and reported to the Office of Under Secretary of Defense Comptroller (OUSD(C)) for inclusion in subsequent budget requests. See DoD 7000.14-R,

Volume 11b, Chapter 55, for more information on inventory and supply management operations as they pertain to Presidential directed drawdowns. As with any other type of drawdown commodity, new contracts are not permitted. Consequently, the type of fuel available for drawdowns will be limited to those available through DESC's existing bulk fuels contracts at the time of drawdown. For example, the FY99 counternarcotics drawdown made available marine diesel F-76 and jet fuel JP-8. Special coordination is required for the transportation, delivery, storage, accountability and distribution of fuel (see Chapter 9 Transportation Planning for more details), generally resulting in a Memorandum of Understanding (MOU) signed by the receiving nation and U.S. Embassy outlining the necessary details.

C4.2.5. Under normal circumstances, the Service tasked with providing specific equipment must fund and ensure the transportation of that equipment to its final destination in accordance with the EXORD. U.S. Transportation Command (USTRANSCOM) is reimbursed for air/sealift provided from the Service tasked with providing the equipment. (See Appendix 2 for more details.)

C4.2.6. Airlift and sealift can be provided using Military Air (MILAIR)/Military Sea (MILSEA) or appropriate time-charter contracts if the scope of existing contracts covers the proposed use (such as time-charter or multiple air mission agreements). Drawdown statutes provide for the supply of commercial transportation and related services acquired by contract for the purposes of the specific drawdown, if the cost to acquire such commercial transportation and related services is less than the cost to the USG of providing such services from existing agency assets.

C4.2.7. Where possible, complete support packages are normally provided for any major end items, to include training for both operation and maintenance of the major end item.

C4.2.8. Basic Security Assistance channels/procedures are used for provision of articles and services.

C4.2.9. Valuation (pricing) process for drawdowns does NOT include Security Assistance surcharges (See Chapter 7).

C4.2.10. Requisitioning of material and spare parts for shipment normally provides authority for use of Force Activity Designator (FAD) levels and priority. Spare parts requisitions are processed on a "Fill or Kill" basis.

C4.2.11. Military/civilian pay and per diem may be included when computing the cost of drawdown services, but only for those funded civilian pay and travel and per diem costs for military and civilian personnel performing an approved support role that is exclusively devoted to the drawdown effort may be included when computing the value of the drawdown services. Examples include personnel tasked to provide specific DoD services for a drawdown, e.g. training teams, personnel conducting equipment repair or refurbishment, personnel deployed in support of the drawdown, quality assurance teams (QAT).

C4.2.12. Unless authorized otherwise, materiel must be provided in condition code "B", or Full Mission Capable (FMC) condition, or -10/-20 standards or better.

C4.2.12.1. U.S. Army Regulation 725-50 (AR 725-50), Table C-38 defines condition code "B - serviceable (issuable with qualification)" as: "new, used, repaired or reconditioned, materiel which is serviceable and issuable for its intended purpose but which is restricted from issue to specific units, activities, or geographical areas by reason of its limited usefulness or short service life expectancy."

C4.2.12.2. FMC as defined by the U.S. Army (DA PAM 750-35 Glossary & AR 700-138), defines equipment and systems that are safe, and have all mission-essential subsystems installed and operating as designated by applicable U.S. Army regulation. This is applicable to all Services. A full mission capable vehicle or system has no faults that are listed in the "not Fully Mission Capable (FMC) ready of" column of the -10/-20 TM PMCS tables that apply to the vehicle/system or its subsystem required by AR 700-138. The terms "ready/available" and "full mission capable" refer to the same status, i.e., equipment is on hand and able to perform its combat missions without endangering the lives of crew or operators.

C4.2.12.3. -10/-20 standards as defined by the US Army (applicable to all services) (DA PAM 750-35 Glossary & AR 750-1, Para 3-1 & 4-6): The following conditions are true of FMC equipment:

C4.2.12.3.1. All faults are identified using the "items to check" column of the applicable TM -10-series and TM –20 series PMCS table.

C4.2.12.3.1.1. Corrective actions that are authorized to be accomplished at unit level, and for which required parts are available, are completed.

C4.2.12.3.1.2. Required parts are requisitioned for faults that require corrective actions.

C4.2.12.3.1.3. Corrective actions that are authorized to be accomplished at a maintenance level above the unit are on a valid direct support maintenance request.

C4.2.12.3.2. Equipment services are performed within the scheduled service interval.

C4.2.12.3.3. All current urgent and limited urgent modification work orders are applied.

C4.2.12.3.4. All authorized basic issue items and components of end item are present and serviceable or on valid requisition.

C4.2.13. Services cannot place a hold/reserve/fence equipment nor spares before the release of DSCA's Execute Order.

C4.3. <u>INTERNAL DSCA RESPONSIBILITIES</u>

The following outlines the internal DSCA responsibilities with regard to drawdowns.

C4.3.1. Country Program Director (CPD) Responsibilities.

C4.3.1.1. Coordinates with the DoS, NSC, DoD offices (including regional/policy offices, Joint Staff and Unified Commands, GC and Comptroller, and the Services), the Security Assistance Organization (SAO), and other government entities to develop drawdown packages, ensuring legal, policy, and logistical requirements are met.

C4.3.1.2. Coordinates draft PD package with GC, OPS-ADMIN, HA/MA and P3-Policy.

C4.3.1.3. Works with the Services to identify available resources for drawdowns, and serves as the "honest broker" to ensure an equitable distribution of requirements amongst the Services to the maximum extent practicable.

C4.3.1.4. Serves as focal point for his/her particular drawdown and coordinates drawdown documentation as required.

C4.3.1.5. Drafts and ensures release of EXORDs granting legal authority and direction for drawdowns to proceed.

C4.3.1.6. Monitors the progress of deliveries and the provision of services under drawdown and ensures that drawdown authority levels are appropriately distributed to accomplish the mission by reviewing monthly Military Department generated delivery reports.

C4.3.1.7. Maintains the "working" file for the drawdown. Upon closure of the drawdown, the official file will be transitioned to and maintained by OPS-ADMIN.

C4.3.2. <u>OPS-ADMIN Responsibilities</u>

C4.3.2.1. Reviews/coordinates draft PD package.

C4.3.2.2. Reviews EXORDs.

C4.3.2.3. Maintains Drawdown Summary spreadsheet on the DSCA P: drive.

C4.3.2.4. Receives monthly delivery reports from the Military Departments for review by OPS-ADMIN and the CPD.

C4.3.2.5. Monitors deliveries to ensure timely reporting by the Services into the DSCA 1000 system.

C4.3.2.6. Identifies any variances between delivered articles and services and the DSCA 1000 system and seeks explanations from the Military Departments as required.

C4.3.2.7. Ensures that overall drawdown ceilings are not exceeded.

C4.3.2.8. Maintains information and databases and tracks authorizations and costs reported by services via the 1000 system and PC-based files.

C4.3.2.9. Prepares annual and adhoc reports to Congress on provision of assistance under drawdown.

C4.3.2.10. Maintains and stores the DSCA historical files for all drawdowns.

C4.3.2.11. Serves as central POC for delivery and reporting issues on drawdowns.

C4.3.3. P3-Policy Responsibilities

C4.3.3.1. Provides general policy guidance regarding drawdowns --- this includes revising/updating the DSCA Drawdown Handbook with additional guidance (e.g., samples of various EXORDs, etc.).

C4.3.3.2. Provides updates to the drawdown section in the Security Assistance Management Manual (SAMM).

C4.3.3.4. Serves as central POC for general questions on drawdowns.

C4.3.3.5. Reviews/coordinates on draft PD packages.

C4.3.3.6. Coordinates with Joint Staff J4 to obtain Project Codes and/or Force Activity Designator (FAD) increases, and termination messages for drawdowns.

C4.3.3.7. Reviews EXORDs to ensure compliance with Security Assistance policy.

C4.3.3.8. Reviews/coordinates on reports or notifications to Congress.

C4.3.3.9. Reviews/coordinates on responses to Congressional inquiries on drawdowns.

C4.3.4. General Counsel Responsibilities

C4.3.4.1. Provides general counsel and advice regarding drawdowns.

C4.3.4.2. Reviews/coordinates on updates to the drawdown section in the Security Assistance Management Manual (SAMM).

C4.3.4.3. Reviews/coordinates on updates to the DSCA Drawdown Handbook.

C4.3.4.4. Serves as central POC for legal issues on drawdowns.

C4.3.4.5. Reviews/coordinates on draft PD packages.

C4.3.4.6. Reviews EXORDs to ensure compliance with the statutory authority.

C4.3.4.7. Reviews/coordinates on reports or notifications to Congress.

C4.3.4.8. Reviews/coordinates on responses to Congressional inquiries on drawdowns.

C4.3.5. <u>Legislative and Public Affairs</u>

C4.3.5.1. Reviews/coordinates on reports or notifications to Congress.

C4.3.5.2. Fields Congressional inquiries on drawdowns.

C5. CHAPTER 5

OVERVIEW OF THE DRAWDOWN PROCESS

C5.1. GENERAL

While no two drawdowns are identical, the following events/steps reflect the significant actions that take place in planning and executing a DoD drawdown. (See slides at Appendix 3).

C5.2. INITIATING CRISIS/POLICY SITUATION

Generally a military/humanitarian crisis occurs or another foreign policy interest is identified in which the drawdown of defense articles/services is an option. The following actions are taken in the interagency process:

C5.2.1 Preliminary identification of potential USG contributions to the situation

C5.2.2 Coordination to determine which foreign policy authorities are appropriate to the situation ((Foreign Military Financing (FMF), Peacekeeping Operations (PKO), Humanitarian Assistance (HA), Drawdown, etc.)).

C5.3. DRAWDOWN PACKAGE DEVELOPMENT

If the Interagency recommends a "drawdown" option for a specific situation, the DSCA has the DoD lead in developing the requirements, costs, and the execution plan of a potential drawdown in conjunction with the Joint Staff, OSD, U.S. Department of State, NSC and the Services. Developing a realistic list of which articles and services are available for drawdown occurs in two parallel processes: an internal DoD process and an interagency process—for which careful and thorough coordination is vital. (See Drawdown Process Charts at Appendix 3.)

C5.3.1. The Interagency process develops supporting documents to notify Congress of the drawdown and prepares the PD for the President's signature.

C5.3.2. In the DoD internal process, the Services estimate the value of the articles and services requested to be provided and assess the potential impact on operational readiness and O&M budget

C5.3.3. Interagency Staffing. (Concurrent with DoD V&A development):

C5.3.3.1. The State Department develops its Congressional notification package on the proposed drawdown with DoD input.

C5.3.3.2. Interagency representatives, working through DoS, often consult informally with Congressional staffers in a "pre-notification consultation" to prepare for Congressional approval of the drawdown.

C5.3.3.3. The Congressional notification package is submitted to the NSC for Presidential review and approval.

C5.3.3.4. Congress is formally notified of the drawdown.

C5.3.3.5. State Department prepares a Memorandum of Justification and drafts the PD for the Drawdown (with DoD input) and submits it to the NSC/White House.

C5.3.3.6. After the required Congressional Notification, the President signs the PD.

C5.3.4. The DoD Internal Process

C5.3.4.1. Where Service(s) and DoD drawdown is considered an option, DSCA tasks the appropriate Service(s) and/or agencies to provide V&A data for defense articles/services identified in the interagency process. In order to expedite the V&A process, DSCA in coordination with Implementing Agencies and organizations (e.g., CECOM, DLA, etc.,) must provide as much information as possible for the required items such as National Stock Number (NSN), DoD Ammunition Codes (DODAC), quantities, sizes, etc. The Services shall not define drawdown requirements. Historically, MILDEP International Logistics Control Offices (ILCO) have been provided with under-defined requirements (e.g. Boots, uniforms, 81mm ammo) and have been expected to cross reference to NSN's/DODACs etc. This is often impossible due to the large variety of similar materiel available in inventory.

C5.3.4.2. V&A data are provided to DSCA with appropriate readiness or Operations & Maintenance (O&M) impact statements. The Services sometimes provide readiness impact statements to DSCA through the Joint Staff.

C5.3.4.3. DSCA coordinates readiness impacts with Joint Staff (if not previously provided through the Joint Staff).

C5.3.4.4. When the Interagency questions the Services' statements of impact on readiness or operations and maintenance, the issue is elevated up the OSD chain for Deputy Secretary of Defense or Secretary of Defense resolution.

C5.3.4.5. The impact of the drawdown on the Services' Operational Readiness (OR) and/or O&M budget is "balanced" among the Services as much as possible until general agreement is reached on the DoD package. This is one of the key roles the DSCA CPD must perform in his/her role as "honest broker," in attempting to "balance the load" among Services.

C5.3.5. Synchronizing Pd Development

The Services normally determine which articles and services are available to support the drawdown during the V&A process. Since the V&A process happens simultaneously with the interagency development of the drawdown package, there is a continual review/update of the drawdown "package." The Interagency determines what is appropriate to provide based on what is actually available (either physically available or can be provided with acceptable Operational Readiness (OR) impact). The final PD should reflect what DoD can, in fact, provide and becomes the base reference for execution of the drawdown.

C5.4. DRAWDOWN EXECUTION

C5.4.1. Before executing a drawdown, the DSCA CPD must have:

C5.4.1.1. A signed copy of the PD.

C5.4.1.2. The State Department's assurance of eligibility (Section 503).

C5.4.1.3. The State Department's assurance that an end-use agreement exists for all drawdown recipients (Section 505).

C5.4.1.4. The State Department's assurance that human rights issues do not preclude delivery of drawdown related equipment and/or services.

C5.4.2. After obtaining the requisite coordination, the DSCA CPD issues an Execute Order(s) authorizing DoD execution of the drawdown.

C5.4.3. Subsequently, the executing Services/DoD Agencies issue their own Execute Order(s) to initiate action to provide the directed equipment or services. This process normally includes:

C5.4.3.1. Providing required maintenance to bring the equipment to the transfer standard (i.e., condition code "B", or FMC), if accomplished with organic assets or within the scope of existing funded contracts

C5.4.3.2. providing spare parts/tools

C5.4.3.3. providing adequate operational and maintenance training if required/applicable and

C5.4.3.4. packing, crating and handling (PC&H) and transportation

C5.4.4. Equipment is staged, consolidated, and containerized at selected sites if required/applicable.

C5.4.5. USTRANSCOM, Military Surface Deployment and Distribution Command (SDDC), and Military Sealift Command (MSC) coordinate Air or Sea transportation and designate Aerial Ports of Embarkation (APOE) or Water Ports of Embarkation (WPOE).

C5.4.6. Shipment is undertaken in one or more iterations as required.

C5.4.7. The DSCA/OSD/Joint Staff monitor the execution of the drawdown and make adjustments as required.

C5.4.8. While the drawdown is being executed, DSCA and the Services shall perform continuous financial reconciliation to ensure all cost elements are reported in a timely manner. Refer to Chapters 10 and 11 for additional information on this process.

C5.4.9. The DSCA provides formal reports to Congress on what articles and services were provided for the drawdown.

C5.4.10. Depending on the nature of the situation, the drawdown process can take as little as 24-48 hours to as much as 2-10 months before the first deliveries begin.

C5.5. TERMINATION OF DRAWDOWN

C5.5.1. Unless otherwise directed by the DSCA CPD, a termination date, not to exceed 18 months from date of Execute Order issuance, will be stated in the Execution Order message.

C5.5.2. The DSCA CPD releases a termination message for closure of the drawdown when all articles and services have been delivered and/or the termination date in the EXORD is reached. (See example Appendix 6).

C5.5.3. Upon receipt of the termination message, OPS-ADMIN shall prepare and release the official notification to Congress (See example Appendix 6).

C5.6. OUT-OF-CHANNEL STARTS - INVALID EQUIPMENT LISTS

C5.6.1. On occasion, individual program advocates within the State Department, OSD, or the NSC policy offices may start developing a concept for a drawdown and prepare a "wish list" of articles and services without full Interagency coordination. The Joint Staff, the Services, and the DSCA CPD may first hear about the proposed drawdown action when a "strawman" is furnished in an Interagency meeting to make "decisions" on the proposed drawdown.

C5.6.2. In such situations, DoD cannot validate at that time whether any of the proposed defense articles and services is available; what, if any, operational impact may come from providing the proposed equipment; or what the associated costs may be. Depending on the level, forum, and associated urgency at which the drawdown proposal is presented, DoD representatives should seek to have the package validated before any decisions are made on the composition of a proposed drawdown.

C5.6.3. Anytime personnel learn that any policy offices are considering a drawdown, it is critically important to get this action into DSCA and Joint Staff channels. Once a "strawman" package has been placed before senior policymakers, it is difficult to make changes. A proper

V&A/OR review must be conducted, even if on an abbreviated time-line, before a drawdown package is presented formally in the Interagency process. It is critical that DoD has the opportunity to ensure that it can support whatever is being developed before a drawdown is formally proposed and reviewed in the Interagency forum.

C6. CHAPTER 6

DRAWDOWN SCOPE AND ELIGIBILITY

C6.1. GENERAL

The documents below, in the order given, provide guidance in determining which types of defense articles and services are authorized to be provided under a specific drawdown.

C6.2. STATUTORY AUTHORITY

The legal authorities invoked for a drawdown (Section 506(a)(1), 506(a)(2), 552(c)(2), or special legislation) may include dollar ceilings, sources of articles and services (e.g. DoD or USG), drawdown recipients, etc.

C6.3. PRESIDENTIAL DETERMINATION (PD)

The PD is the official document authorizing a drawdown execution. The Department of Defense is not authorized to initiate provision of services or requisition/deliver equipment until the PD is signed. The DSCA CPD must have a signed copy of the PD before releasing the EXORD. The PD is normally a one-page document that states the recipients for the drawdown, cites appropriate statutory authority, and gives a general description of the types of defense articles/services to be provided along with the purpose for which the articles and services are to be provided. The PD also states a dollar ceiling for the drawdown. The PD number from the authorizing document shall be cited in all EXORDs and other correspondence relative to drawdowns. Copies of recent PD's can be found on the World Wide Web at the Federal Register document research page, http://www.access.gpo.gov/su_docs/aces/aces140.html. (See Appendix 4 for an example).

C6.4. PRESIDENTIAL DETERMINATION (PD) STAFFING SUPPORT PAPERS

The State Department and the NSC normally develop a series of memos as part of the PD development package. These documents provide additional clarification of the intended purpose and scope of the drawdown and usually provide an initial list of the equipment/services originally planned to be provided under the drawdown. These documents are normally staffed with DoD (OSD, Joint Staff and DSCA) representatives before completion. The "Memorandum of Justification" is essential to the DoD in deciding what does and does not fit within the scope of an individual drawdown. (See the sample Memorandum of Justification at Appendix 4).

C6.5. RECIPIENT ELIGIBILITY

The proposed recipients for drawdown may be countries or entities that previously were not eligible for receipt of US defense articles and services under the Foreign Assistance Act (FAA) or the Arms Export Control Act. As DoD proceeds with its development of a potential drawdown package, close coordination is required with the State Department to ensure that the appropriate FAA Section 503 and determinations of eligibility have been completed. In addition, an FAA Section 505 agreement must also be signed by the recipient country/entity. In the past, PD's for drawdowns have been signed prior to completion of the eligibility agreements or the 505 agreements, but delivery could not be executed until these requirements are met. The DSCA EXORD for the drawdown must not be issued until the PD is signed, and actual delivery cannot be made until the entire eligibility legal structure is in place (FAA, Section 503/FAA, Section 505 agreement).

C7. CHAPTER 7

DEVELOPMENT OF A DRAWDOWN PACKAGE

C7.1. GENERAL

As noted earlier, there is no "standard" drawdown because the level of urgency and policy goals are different for each one. However, drawdown package development generally follows the following procedure.

C7.2. DEVELOPMENT OF A DRAWDOWN PACKAGE

C7.2.1. Request for V&A data.

C7.2.2. Review of V&A data and impact on operational readiness (OR) and/or O&M funding.

C7.2.3. Interagency review and refinement of the proposed drawdown package.

C7.2.4. Updated V&A (multiple times if necessary).

C7.2.5. Completion of the PD.

C7.3. REQUEST FOR VALUATION AND AVAILABILITY (V&A) DATA

C7.3.1. Definition. Valuation and Availability (V&A) data estimates reflect rough order magnitude data, provided for planning purposes, showing projected availabilities and estimated values for requested drawdown defense articles or services. To avoid confusion with FMS case preparation process, the term Price and Availability (P&A) data should not be used in reference to data developed for execution of a drawdown.

C7.3.2. Basic V&A Data Request. As preliminary requirements for the drawdown are identified (including NSNs, sizes, quantity etc), the DSCA CPD forwards the list(s) to the Defense Logistics Agency/ Services/ Action Officer(s)/program managers, to obtain V&A data for proposed equipment and services from their respective ILCO. The DSCA CPD should request the Services/Defense Agencies to clearly identify the value of ALL potential and allowable equipment and services associated with the drawdown. The Service Action Officer/program managers should follow the Total Package Approach (TPA) concept by specifically requesting the following information in table C7.T1:

Table C7.T1. Basic V&A Data Request

Step	Projected Costs	Potential/Allowable Cost
1	Drawdown value of equipment.	
2	Projected value of "in-house" capability to repair/refurbish any candidate equipment to the transfer standard (i.e. condition code "B", or -10/-20 standards, or Full Mission Capable (FMC) or better).	
3	Projected value for any required training associated with equipment not previously purchased or provided to the drawdown recipient.	
4	Projected value of any proposed training for the drawdown that is NOT tied to specific equipment being provided under the drawdown.	
5	Projected value for any required spare parts or special tools or equipment to support the candidate equipment (normally 6-months to 1-year package).	
6	Projected packing, crating, and handling (PC&H) associated with shipment of the equipment and support materials	
7	Projected transportation values associated with each major item or support equipment.	
8	Projected value for providing any non-training DoD services under the drawdown –normally the value of civilian pay (where appropriate), travel/deployment value, per diem, etc.	

C7.3.3. The time given to the Services/Defense Agencies for development of this data will be directly proportional to the urgency of the drawdown. Depending on time-sensitivity, much of the preliminary coordination for V&A data and interagency identification of requirements may be accomplished on an informal "Action Officer" level. However, informal requests and answers need to be followed up with formal taskers and formal answers as soon as possible -- particularly if it looks like items are going to be contentious. Things are generally moving fast and informal commitment to host countries or international organizations may not be "remembered." All must remember V&A data represents a condition valid for a specific point in time in the supply system and becomes outdated the moment it is provided. Hence, changes should be expected by the time a PD is signed, 505 agreements are in place and Execute Orders are issued.

C7.3.4. "Drawdownable" versus " Non-drawdownable" Services. In responding to the DSCA request for V&A data, the Services/Defense Agencies should clearly identify what, if any, of the costs associated with the requested V&A data are NOT "drawdownable." As noted in the Introduction and Chapter 4, no new contracting or procurement is authorized in executing a drawdown. If, due to the lack of existing "in-house" capabilities, providing any specific equipment/services (for example, repair/refurbishment, training, installation, transportation, etc.) is not possible under the drawdown authority, this needs to be identified early. If an alternate source cannot be identified for those "non-drawdownable" services, the proposed items associated with these services should not be considered as valid candidates for the drawdown. End items should not be provided unless the support (logistics/training) necessary to make the end items fully operational will be available to the drawdown recipient.

C7.3.5. Value of Drawdown Equipment/Services. Valuation of equipment and services will follow pricing policies prescribed in Chapter 7 of the DoD FMR 7000.14R, Volume 15, for defense articles issued from stock and personnel services. See C11.2.1. for more details.

C7.3.6. Operational Readiness Impact. Service V&A data should also identify if there is any operational readiness (OR) impact associated with the provision of equipment and services. If an OR impact is identified, review and comment by the Joint Staff is mandatory. See paragraph C7.2.4. for more details.

C7.4. DOD REVIEW OF V&A DATA AND OR IMPACT

C7.4.1. DSCA Initial Review. Upon receipt of the Service/Defense Agency V&A data, the responsible DSCA CPD consolidates the input from all sources to make an initial list of the articles and services reasonably available for the drawdown. This initial review should make a preliminary assessment of the completeness/validity of the provided V&A data to ensure the provided information, in fact, "answers the mail." If necessary, DSCA personnel should request supplemental data from the appropriate Service/Defense Agency. If high visibility or priority items are indicated not to be available or reported to have significant adverse OR impact, additional discussion with the Service may be warranted to ensure that a full Service position has been coordinated. Initial DSCA review of V&A data will normally result in a "strawman" list of proposed drawdown equipment and services. This list may frequently turn into the initial allocation of taskings for the drawdown.

C7.4.2. OSD, Joint Staff, and Service Review of Proposed List. DSCA CPD will normally circulate this initial candidate list of equipment and services to the appropriate OSD International Security Affairs (ISA), International Security Policy (ISP), Special Operations Low Intensity Conflict (SOLIC), Joint Staff and Service Staffs for either informal or formal review to get general comments as DoD establishes a consensus on what equipment/services will be presented to the Interagency. Where there are contentious items, either internal to DoD, or between DoD or other departments, formal staffing is more likely to be required.

C7.4.3. Joint Staff Coordination. The Joint Staff J4 Sustainment & International Logistics Division (SILD) is the focal point for Joint Staff coordination of drawdown actions. In addition, the Joint Staff J5 is usually represented at initial State and OSD policy discussions related to the regional crisis for which the drawdown is being considered. Getting Joint Staff on board early and keeping them up to date will save problems later.

C7.4.4. <u>Operational Readiness (OR) Impact</u>. When a Service or Defense Agency identifies a significant OR impact associated with the provision of any equipment or services, the DSCA turns to the Joint Staff to validate the Service analysis. The OR impact statements may be provided directly to DSCA as a part of the Service's V&A data or provided to the Joint Staff by the Service. (NOTE: Army provides any V&A data with OR impact through the Joint Staff to DSCA). The Department of Defense excludes items or services from drawdowns for which the Services have provided significant operational impact. Where critical or mission-essential items are identified with significant OR impact, DSCA, OSD, and the Joint Staff will need to develop a formal DoD position on providing these items. In the past, one OR impact for Colombia had to be resolved at the Deputy Secretary of Defense – Secretary of the Army level. Staffing time increases appreciably when such high level decision-makers become involved.

C7.4.5. <u>O&M Impact</u>. Increasingly, the O&M cost of diversion of funds from other activities is being identified as the adverse OR impact for a given drawdown, rather than any specific OR impact due to loss of the equipment or provision of the services. DSCA will coordinate with OSD and the Joint Staff in reviewing Service impact statements. A possible solution may be to task another Service to provide an item/service when more than one Service is capable of meeting the requirement.

C7.5. <u>INTERAGENCY REVIEW AND REFINEMENT OF MATERIAL AND SERVICES PROPOSED FOR DRAWDOWN</u>

With completion of the DoD review, the proposed drawdown list is provided to the Interagency for review, this may be accomplished through formal coordination or informal review. Contentious or sensitive issues may dictate formal coordination as determined by a DSCA regional director. Based on Interagency review, the drawdown list will either be agreed to or modified.

C7.6. <u>UPDATED V&A DATA</u>

Based on the results of the interagency review, DSCA may go back to the Services to request additional or clarifying V&A data. Again, this may be either a formal or an informal update of the previously provided data. As a minimum, informal re-validation of V&A data for any items remaining on the proposed list after interagency review is critical.

C7.7. <u>COMPLETION OF THE PRESIDENTIAL DETERMINATION (PD)</u>

Based on general Interagency consensus on the proposed drawdown package, the State Department completes development of the PD for the drawdown. This includes drafting the proposed PD itself, developing the Memorandum of Justification and any required Congressional notification package. The PD package will normally be coordinated with OSD, DSCA, and Joint Staff. If the Memorandum of Justification includes a general description of the equipment and services to be provided, the DSCA CPD should ensure that this is an accurate listing. (See sample Memorandum of Justification, Appendix 4).

C7.8. MULTIPLE V&A DATA CYCLES

Particularly with non-emergency drawdowns, there may be two or more V&A data/package development cycles. There will normally be an initial package developed and an Execute Order issued to initiate the drawdown as quickly as possible. Usually, subsequent EXORDs will be issued, as projected values for initial deliveries are reconciled. For emergency drawdowns, there will usually only be 1-3 EXORDs. As noted before, the drawdown ends when the agreed items are delivered and costs reported and termination date is reached. For non-emergency drawdowns, there is likely to be increased push for reconciliation of actual costs and supplemental requests for equipment if residual authority remains.

C7.9. PACKAGE DEVELOPMENT TIMELINES

As discussed earlier, the drawdown package development can be as short as a week or as much as 7-10 months. The timeline discussed above will be compressed or expanded to meet these requirements.

C8. CHAPTER 8

EXECUTION PLANNING

C8.1. EXECUTION PLANNING

As consensus on the drawdown is being completed, the DSCA CPD needs to start coordination for execution of the drawdown and development of the EXORD. Key planning considerations and items for coordination are: Completion/General Consensus on the Drawdown Package, Balancing of Service Taskings, Project Code, Force Activity Designator level, Maintenance/Repair Standards, Execution lead-times, Collection and Consolidation Point (CCP), Designation of a Service Lead, Assignment of Service RCNs, and Transportation Planning. Transportation planning has an entire set of considerations that are covered in more detail in Chapter 9. A sample EXORD is included at Appendix 6.

C8.2. COMPLETION OF DRAWDOWN PACKAGE

Final agreement on the drawdown package may not occur until the day the EXORD is released. If there is not complete agreement on the total package, the initial Execute Order may only provide initial tasking to start the drawdown.

C8.3. BALANCING OF SERVICE TASKINGS

As interagency agreement on what will be provided is completed, DSCA is responsible for allocating tasks to the Military Services and Defense Agencies. Where only one Service or Agency can provide a specific item or service, this is an easy allocation. Where more than one Service/Agency can provide items/services, DSCA will normally seek to "balance the load." Balancing the load may take into consideration the current drawdown, and the drawdown taskings given to each Service/Agency during other recent or ongoing drawdowns. For common-use DLA-managed items/material, (spare parts, uniforms, system batteries, etc.), any Service or Agency can be tasked to provide the items and bear related O&M cost, even though another Service or Agency would normally be considered the "item manager."

C8.4. PROJECT CODE

All drawdowns require a three-digit alphanumeric project code to support execution. This code will be included in all requisitions and shipping documents. DSCA P3, with the DSCA CPDs, (see Chapter C4.3.3.6), coordinates with J4 Sustainment and International Logistics Division (SILD) for assignment of the drawdown project code. This project code will be included in the EXORD(s). J4-SILD project codes are valid for a period not to exceed 1 year but can be revalidated in up to 1-year increments on a case-by-case basis until the drawdown is complete.

Whenever necessary, DSCA P3, with the DSCA CPDs can request J4 SILD to extend drawdown project code validity before its expiration date.

C8.5. FORCE ACTIVITY DESIGNATOR (FAD) LEVEL

DSCA P3, with the DSCA CPDs, (see Chapter C4.3.3.6), coordinates with J4 SILD to confirm or get assignment of the FAD level, which provides the appropriate priority for requisitioning and shipping of drawdown equipment. Where the drawdown is to an established FMS customer, the country's existing FAD may be used or, if the "urgency of need" priority for the drawdown is deemed to be higher than that provided under the existing FAD, DSCA/P3 can coordinate a higher FAD level for the drawdown. Where the drawdown recipient does not have an existing FAD, DSCA/P3, with the DSCA CPD, establishes one with J4 SILD. In addition to FAD level, the drawdown EXORD will normally include guidance that the Services and DLA should fill the drawdown requisitions as if they are being filled for U.S. forces. This places the drawdown requisitions at a higher priority and eliminates the problem of non-fill of blanket order FMS requisitions below the "reorder point" from Service stocks. FAD level and "U.S. fill" guidance should be included in the EXORD.

C8.6. MAINTENANCE/REPAIR STANDARDS

The DSCA CPD needs to coordinate with the Services and the Interagency to confirm the required maintenance/repair standard for the equipment to be delivered. As a general rule, the minimum standard for delivery of equipment is Full Mission Capable (FMC) or applicable Service standard for special equipment (see Chapter C4.2.12). Aircraft transfer standards are normally higher and would be utilized for any assets to be transferred in flyable condition. If a standard less than FMC is proposed, all parties (Interagency, Services, and proposed recipient) must understand the political implications of delivering equipment in less than FMC condition. This is NOT recommended and DSCA, in general, does not support such delivery unless the recipient already has similar equipment and has an existing repair capability. Where the urgency of the drawdown precludes completing full pre-delivery maintenance, all parties need to understand the condition of the equipment. While some U.S. and host country policy personnel may push for quick delivery over delivery of mission capable equipment, there is a high probability that the USG will subsequently be criticized by the recipient for delivery of non-mission capable equipment -- Any decision to deliver less than FMC equipment must be carefully weighed and fully coordinated with implementing agencies and organizations.

C8.7. SPARE PARTS AND SUPPORT EQUIPMENT

As discussed earlier, (see Chapter 4) the goal is to use the Total Package Approach (TPA) concept in delivering drawdown equipment. The drawdown package should include provisions for spare parts, special tools and necessary support equipment. Depending on the nature of the drawdown, the target for spare parts should be a one-year spare package. Delivery of end items without associated spare parts and support equipment should be considered only when the recipient already has the same equipment and an established support capability. For example, consideration should be given to provision of adequate batteries for battery-operated equipment - particularly communications equipment. Where rechargeable batteries are provided or electrically operated equipment is provided, Action Officer's need to ensure the U.S.-provided charging equipment or power converter systems are 220V systems, NOT 110V systems. Any consideration to deliver equipment without support equipment, spares or expendable supplies, such as batteries, again needs to be weighed against urgency of need, Service impact statements, and the political embarrassment due to our delivering equipment that ceases to operate shortly after arrival. The DSCA CPD, in coordination with other interested parties can make the ultimate decision regarding spare parts.

C8.8. EXECUTION LEAD-TIMES

C8.8.1. The triggers which authorize DoD to expend O&M funds and /or to start collection, repair and shipment of drawdown items are signature of the PD for the drawdown, State Department confirmation of Section 503 eligibility, Section 505 end-use agreements, human rights vetting, by State Department and release of the DoD EXORD. Outside pressure to commence your drawdown is likely to increase at this point. It is important to reiterate, that DoD starts drawdown only when the PD is signed and the EXORD is issued. Timeliness of deliveries is important. As the drawdown "package" has been generally discussed for some period (anywhere from 2 weeks to 2/3 months), there is frequently an interagency perspective that the drawdown material will be delivered "tomorrow" once the PD is signed. In emergency drawdown situations and/or drawdowns with DLA managed common items, the normal lead-time to collect equipment and prepare it for shipment is 3-5 weeks depending on the volume and nature of the equipment. The EXORD should take this lead-time into consideration in designating the Required Delivery Date (RDD).

C8.8.2. Maintenance/Repair Lead-Times. A second factor that affects delivery lead-time is the degree to which any repair or refurbishment is required to bring equipment to the established maintenance transfer standard (FMC or as otherwise designated). Maintenance lead-times vary (e.g., from 60-120 days), depending on the condition of the equipment and the status of "in-house" maintenance capabilities. If there are significant differences between repair lead-times for items, consideration may need to be given to multiple shipments.

C8.9. USE OF COLLECTION AND CONSOLIDATION POINT (CCP)

If the drawdown consists of a large number of major end items, spare parts and support equipment, and particularly if this equipment is to be provided from more than one Service, consideration should be given to the use of a CCP. If this is appropriate, the DSCA CPD should coordinate with the Services and DLA to agree on a site that is located to support collection and onward movement for subsequent shipment.

C8.10. ASSIGNMENT OF RECORD CONTROL NUMBER (RCN)

The RCN is assigned by OPS-ADMIN., In conjunction with the Country Code and Fiscal Year (FY) of a drawdown, it identifies a unique record in the DSCA 1000 System, and is also used in MILSTRIP documentation. This unique record identifies a specific commodity or specific service to be provided via the drawdown to another country or international organization. The RCN, entered in record positions 2-5 of the DSCA 1000 System, is always a four-digit code (2 alpha, 2 numeric) in which the first two digits must always be alpha characters and the third and fourth digits must always be numeric. Based on the number and types for different equipment or services tasked, each Service/Agency should be allocated adequate blocks of RCNs to support reporting within the DSCA 1000 System. For more details, see Chapter 11, section C11.6.

C8.10.1. Same Country/Same FY. Once a set of RCNs has been assigned for a country within a particular FY, any new drawdowns with new PD's, for that same country within that same FY, must use a new set of RCNs for each new drawdown within the same FY.

C8.10.2. Same Country/Different FY. Drawdowns for the same country, but in different FYs, can actually use the same RCN series, per each different FY. It does not matter when the data is actually entered into the DSCA 1000 System, provided the FYs are different for each set of data.

C8.11. FISCAL YEAR OF A DRAWDOWN

Drawdown executions may span more than one fiscal year. For tracking and reporting purposes, to ensure accuracy and consistency, the FY of a drawdown is the FY in which the PD is signed or the special legislative authority is invoked, regardless of when the commodities and services are actually drawn down or actually delivered, and regardless of when the data is actually entered into the DSCA 1000 System. For drawdowns being executed over several years, data should be entered against the original FY of the drawdown.

C9. CHAPTER 9

TRANSPORTATION PLANNING

C9.1. TRANSPORTATION PLANNING

As a potential drawdown is under development, early "heads up" notification to transportation offices and early coordination as requirements gel is essential to ensure that the transportation agencies (USTRANSCOM, SDDC, AMC, and MSC) can meet the desired policy requirements. When a PD and an EXORD are finally issued, external pressure will build for delivery "yesterday." Coordination with USTRANSCOM, SDDC and MSC should be undertaken at every stage in the process.

C9.2. EXISTING AIRLIFT/SEALIFT ASSETS

Transportation planning for drawdowns is restricted to the use of DoD airlift and sealift assets unless the cost to acquire such commercial transportation and related services is less than the cost to the USG of providing such services from existing agency assets. Use of DoD military-owned/-leased aircraft or use of SDDC contracted ships under long-term time charter. SDDC has cargo ships available on long-term charter worldwide that can be used to for drawdown shipments. Long-term "open" contract arrangements for commercial aircraft are not as common, but can be used if the scope of the existing contracts meets the "no new contracting /no new procurement" restrictions. Early coordination with USTRANSCOM and SDDC may permit "contingency" planning of available shipping assets. SDDC may be able to consider the anticipated drawdown requirement as they assign transportation missions to charter ships such that the shipping is readily available when the drawdown is executed.

C9.3. PREPARATION AND TRANSPORT TO APOE/WPOE (AERIAL/WATER PORT OF EMBARKATION)

C9.3.1. Cargo Preparation. Services and Agencies providing equipment are responsible for pre-shipment inspection of all cargo to ensure it is complete and in Full Mission Capable (FMC) status, unless a lesser equipment standard has been agreed to.

C9.3.2. CONUS Origination. SDDC undertakes appropriate action to coordinate movement from origin to WPOE/APOEs. Services/Agencies, in coordination with SDDC, are responsible for movement of drawdown cargo from source depots to the designated WPOEs/APOEs. SDDC has the lead for coordination of CONUS movements. Established transportation networks and procedures will be used for this movement. Where a specific Service has been designated as lead Service for collecting cargo, it will coordinate delivery of other Service cargo to the lead Service designated consolidation point (See paragraph C9.4.3). All ammunition requirements from all Services will be coordinated through the Joint Munitions Transportation Coordinating Activity (JMTCA) at Rock Island Arsenal IL.

C9.3.3. <u>OCONUS Origination</u>. Where drawdown cargo originates from OCONUS sites, SDDC does not have the established networks for line haul service and the Combatant Command and Service component transportation offices pick up this mission.

C9.3.4. <u>Special Cargo Requirements</u>. If any cargo requires special handling (containerization, refrigeration, sensitive item security controls, ammunition compatibility, etc.), the Services and transportation offices need to identify this as early as possible to ensure appropriate funding and coordination is accomplished.

C9.4. <u>AIRLIFT VERSUS SEALIFT</u>

The decision to use airlift versus sealift will generally depend on the urgency of the drawdown, the nature of the drawdown cargo (size/volume), and the value of drawdown authority assigned.

C9.4.1. Use https://sms.transcom.mil/sms-perl/SMSWEBStart.pl to estimate airlift costs. No special permission required, just annotate airport locator code of origin and destination and type of aircraft to obtain a Special Assignment Airlift Mission (SAAM) cost estimate. If you want an AMC channel airlift cost that is possible also. Tonnage estimates (ACL) for aircraft type are in AFP 10-1403, Air Mobility Planning Factors, and table 3, Aircraft Payloads. Actually, more aircraft will be needed. The table lists 89 tons for a C-5 yet during Desert Shield/Storm, 50 tons was achieved more often. Distance requires fuel, which adds weight, which decreases tons airlifted. There is a limit on air refueling aircraft. Also, overseas over flight restrictions may increase the flight duration.

C9.4.2. Surface movement can be less expensive, but due to the limited quantities of ships on long-term charter arrangements, movement of the drawdown cargo may be restricted to availability of shipping. If the drawdown consists of large equipment or a large volume of equipment, surface movement may be the only cost effective solution. Dependent on the nature of the equipment and urgency of the drawdown, consideration may be given to splitting the shipment between airlift and surface.

C9.5. <u>STANDARD AIRLIFT VERSUS SPECIAL ASSIGNMENT AIRLIFT MISSION (SAAM)</u>

C9.5.1. <u>Existing Networks</u>. If airlift is considered for movement, the degree of urgency and the existence of (or lack of) Air Mobility Command (AMC) channel or other programmed flights to the final destination will dictate whether Special Assignment Airlift Mission (SAAM) procedures and costs need to used for the drawdown. If an existing network is in place, DSCA and the tasked Services can take advantage and ship the drawdown cargo at minimum airlift cost on established routes. When ammunition is involved, each Service is responsible for obtaining required air clearances. As an alternative, cargo can be shipped as far forward as existing routes can support and SAAM lift used for the last portion of the delivery.

C9.5.2. <u>Cargo Control</u>. The use of SAAM flights can be more expensive but it permits maximum control of the cargo movement. When multiple cargo items being shipped for the drawdown are put in the "standard" AMC routes for delivery, close tracking is required by Service and DSCA OPS-ADMIN personnel to maintain visibility of the cargo. Cargo visibility is easily lost and confirmation of delivery can be complicated. Use of consolidated SAAM movement provides maximum cargo control. The JMTCA is the validator for ammunition SAAM requests for all Services.

C9.6. ARRIVAL PLANNING - WPODS /APODS (WATER/AERIAL PORTS OF DEBARKATION) AND ONWARD MOVEMENT

C9.6.1. <u>WPOD Reception Capabilities -- Augmentation</u>. In selecting in-country WPOD/APODs, transportation agencies need to ensure facilities at those locations can accommodate the planned ships or aircraft (particularly in remote areas). If there are physical deficiencies at the planned reception site, but it is deemed as the only feasible site to support the mission, DoD assets may be used to augment the capability of military cargo handling equipment, personnel and units (e.g., Movement Control Teams, airfield repair assets, deployable air control assets, etc). If augmentation is required, the cost of this effort must be programmed within the overall ceilings for that drawdown. On a related note, DoD, DoS or recipient site augmentation may be required because DoD has no existing contractual arrangements in the region or site to perform reception, offload, or control services. In those cases, the possibility of obtaining contract funding from interagency sources (e.g. DoS) for WPOD/APOD reception should be explored.

C9.6.2. <u>Reception and Onward Movement of Cargo – U.S. or Recipient</u>. Early in the planning process, agreement needs to be made between the U.S. representatives, the recipient and any third party participants (UN, NATO, non-governmental agencies, etc.) regarding who will be responsible for receipt and onward movement of the cargo once it has arrived at the designated receiving waterport or airport. Generally, if the WPOD/APOD is located in the country of final destination, anticipate the cargo will be turned over to the appropriate in-country representatives. If the USG retains responsibility for onward movement, then the USG responsibility for cargo movement transitions from SDDC to the Combatant Command's designated transportation offices.

C9.6.3. <u>Quality Assurance Teams (QAT)</u>. Planning for all major deliveries (major end items, sensitive items, etc.) should include the allocation of drawdown authority (i.e., salary/per diem) for quality assurance teams to verify that all shipped cargo has been delivered and that the items and/or services are complete. Full operational checks at the delivery site may be required depending on the nature of equipment handover. As noted above, Services are responsible for ensuring that all equipment is fully operational and inspected for completeness before shipment.

C9.7. TRANSPORTATION PLANNING ITEMS

C9.7.1. <u>Transportation Account Codes (TAC)</u>. Early Service establishment of TAC codes will facilitate USTRANSCOM, SDDC planning. For sealift movements, SDDC may require a MIPR of funds from responsible Services. Service transportation offices should establish and forward the applicable codes and be prepared to execute any required MIPRs. The TAC provides the long line of accounting to include the ESP code so the billing can be identified to the specific PD for payment and subsequent reporting to the DSCA 1000 system.

C9.7.2. <u>APOE/APOD and WPOE/WPOD Designation</u>. USTRANSCOM and/or SDDC should identify the applicable Aerial Ports of Embarkation/Debarkation (APOE/APOD) and Water Ports of Embarkation/Debarkation (WPOE/WPOD) as early as possible. Wherever possible, this information should be included in the initial Execute Order to facilitate Service execution.

C9.7.3. <u>DODAAC/MAPAD Designation</u>. DSCA and USTRANSCOM/SDDC will coordinate as early as possible to identify the applicable DoD Activity Address Code (DODAAC) and Military Assistance Program Address Directory (MAPAD) for delivery of the drawdown equipment. When the drawdown recipient has established DODAAC/MAPAD addresses, coordination should be undertaken with the SAO to select one of the existing addresses or to create new ones. When there is no existing DODAAC, MAPAD DSCA CPD/Services, will need to acquire the necessary information and build the necessary information and address codes. This should be included in the EXORD.

C9.7.4. <u>CCP Designation</u>. As previously noted, if a CCP is planned to support the drawdown, this information needs to be identified to USTRANSCOM, SDDC as early as possible and should be included in the Execute Order.

C9.7.5. <u>Required Delivery Dates (RDD)</u>. Based on lead-times required established for collection and packing of material and the political urgency of delivery, the EXORD should clearly establish the Required Delivery Dates (RDD). The RDD is the d ate cargo should arrive at the final destination). For multiple shipment and multiple modes (air/sea) the EXORDs may identify multiple RDDs.

C9.7.6. <u>Transportation Control Number (TCN) / Transportation Control and Movement Document (TCMD) During Execution Phase</u>. During the execution phase, DSCA and Service Action Officer's should obtain TCN and TCMD numbers for high-priority/high-visibility items to permit tracking of the cargo. This is particularly helpful in the case of airlift shipments in order to track movement of the items. USTRANSCOM has databases that can be used to locate and track most cargo with a TCN number. Before shipping ammunition items, Services will submit Advanced Transportation Control Movement Documents (ATCMD).

C9.8. <u>FUEL TRANSPORTATION, DELIVERY, AND DISTRIBUTION</u>

Prior or during execution DSCA CPDs will insure MILDEP Action Officer's, SAO and Defense Energy Support Center (DESC) coordinate transportation, delivery and distribution of fuel. These operations require close coordination among all players due to the special nature and costs associated with transport, and the logistics/infrastructure considerations required for unloading, storage, and distribution monitoring. The following should be considered.

C9.8.1. <u>Transportation</u>. Transportation cost for fuel is a significant consideration. If fuel transport is part of the drawdown Services will have to pay, transportation costs up front with their O&M funds. Depending on the quantity of fuel and points of loading/unloading, the cost for transportation may exceed the cost of fuel itself. DESC will work with the Services to ensure the required funds are in place to contract for the fuel and to secure the tanker assets needed to transfer the fuel. DESC will determine the most efficient supply point, route, tanker/barge availability and transfer dates taking into consideration the receiving nation's capabilities.

C9.8.2. <u>Delivery</u>. DESC, in conjunction with the country team, will conduct a survey of the country's infrastructure to ensure the delivery/unloading/storage of fuel can take place efficiently. A Memorandum of Understanding (MOU) will be drafted and signed between the receiving nation and U.S. Embassy outlining the necessary details.

C9.8.3. <u>Distribution</u>. Due to high risk of misuse of fuel once it is delivered to the receiving nation, DSCA CPDs will work closely with in country Action Officer's to ensure fuel end-usage monitoring procedures are in place to reduce the risk of misuse. End Use Monitoring procedures need to be agreed up-front with the receiving nation, and can be documented in a separate MOU.

C10. CHAPTER 10

DRAWDOWN EXECUTION

C10.1. DRAWDOWN EXECUTION

DSCA is responsible for issuing the DoD Execute Order and supervising execution of the drawdown. Based on the drawdown policies/guidelines and planning considerations identified in the earlier chapters, DSCA CPD should develop the Execute Order along the guidelines indicated below and conduct follow-on supervision/monitoring of execution. For emergency drawdowns in particular, the DSCA CPD must ensure that the EXORDs contain firm and specific requirements for materiel and services. For non-emergency situations and or drawdowns involving multiple countries, there will be an initial package developed and an EXORD issued with general supply/financial guidance to initiate the drawdown as quickly as possible. Subsequent EXORDs will be issued as additional countries sign section 505 agreements, requirement lists are firmed up, and projected costs for initial deliveries are reconciled.

C10.2. EXECUTE ORDER DEVELOPMENT

C10.2.1. Timing. The interagency will expect release of the drawdown Execute Order concurrent with signature of the PD for the drawdown. In order to accomplish this, the "final" version of the EXORD should be put into Interagency staffing by the DSCA CPD approximately 5-7 days before the expected signature of the PD (Note this is frequently a very "soft" date depending when State forwards the PD to the NSC who forwards it to the President). Joint Staff frequently requires 4-5 days minimum to complete its internal staffing and waits until it has seen Service comments before completing Joint Staff planning (particularly if any of the Services are expected to surface any OR impact issues). This can increase staffing time by an additional 3-5 days. In the case of "real" crisis drawdowns, these lead-times will likely be reduced.

C10.2.2. Execute Order Composition. The initial DSCA EXORD for any drawdown should include the following information as applicable, to preclude the need to issue supplemental instructions:

C10.2.2.1. Authority for the Drawdown (Legislation and PD) for DWCF.

C10.2.2.1.1. Service Taskings (by Service/Agency):

C10.2.2.1.1.1. Clear delineation of what is to be provided (include National Stock Number (NSN), quantity, sizes etc).

C10.2.2.1.1.2. Any Service unique instructions.

C10.2.2.1.2. Coordinating Instructions:

C10.2.2.1.2.1. Drawdown Project Code.

C10.2.2.1.2.2. Authorized FAD.

C10.2.2.1.2.3. Maintenance/Repair Standard.

C10.2.2.1.2.4. Training / Spare Parts / Support Equipment Requirement (if not already covered)

C10.2.2.1.2.5. Spare Parts Requisitioning Guidance:

C10.2.2.1.2.5.1. Fill as for US Forces.

C10.2.2.1.2.5.2. "Fill or Kill" requisitions.

C10.2.2.1.2.6. Allocation of Service RCN.

C10.2.2.1.2.7. Allocation of "Not to Exceed" dollar value of drawdown authority allocated to each Service / Defense Agency (Based on projected costs provided by each tasked agency).

C10.2.2.1.2.8. Identification of Basic Drawdown Policies:

C10.2.2.1.2.8.1 No new contracting or procurement except for transportation.

C10.2.2.1.2.8.2. Reimbursement of DWCF provided equipment/services.

C10.2.2.1.2.8.3. Tasked Service funds movement to final destination, and report total Services costs, all deliveries and undelivered values into the DSCA 1000 System.

C10.2.2.1.3. Transportation Instructions:

C10.2.2.1.3.1. RDD(s).

C10.2.2.1.3.2. CCP / QAT(s) (if applicable).

C10.2.2.1.3.3. Applicable APOE/WPOE(s).

C10.2.2.1.3.4. Applicable APOD/WPOD(s).

C10.2.2.1.3.5. Any special transportation instructions.

C10.2.2.1.3.6. DODAAC and MAPAD address codes.

C10.2.2.1.3.7. Any delivery or handling instructions at delivery locations.

C10.2.2.1.4. Termination Instructions: As indicated in paragraph C5.5, unless otherwise directed, a termination date not to exceed 18 months from date of execute order issuance will be stated.

C10.2.2.1.5. POC phone and fax numbers.

C10.3. EXECUTE ORDER COORDINATION

Execute Orders are normally coordinated with the following offices and staffs:

C10.3.1. State PM-RSAT.

C10.3.2. State Regional Bureau.

C10.3.3. OSD Policy Office (ISA, ISP or SOLIC).

C10.3.4. Tasked Services.

C10.3.5. Tasked Agencies.

C10.3.6. Joint Staff (J4 Logistics Directorate), Sustainment & International Logistics Division (SILD) as the lead division office).

C10.3.7. USTRANSCOM (either info or coordinating copies to SDDC and MSC).

C10.3.8. Applicable Combatant Command.

C10.3.9. Internal DSCA (GC, P3, OPS-ADMIN and BUS-OPS).

C10.4. POST-EXECUTE ORDER RELEASE ACTIONS

With release of the initial EXORD for the drawdown, DSCA and Service Action Officer's can anticipate the following actions/requirements:

C10.4.1. Issuance of supplemental Service EXORDs (Service Action Officer's).

C10.4.1.1. Clarification of EXORD guidance (as required).

C10.4.1.2. Monitoring status of Service/Agency execution status.

C10.4.1.3. Resolution of any policy and execution issues.

C10.4.1.4. Continued development of drawdown package if full authority was not allocated in the initial EXORD.

C10.4.1.5. Issuance of supplemental EXORDs, as required.

C10.4.1.6. Reminding OSD and State policy offices of the agreed upon lead-times.

C10.5. DSCA MONITORING

After release of the EXORD, DSCA CPD will spend most of his/her time in the above actions, particularly asking the Services for status reports. Acquisition of appropriate TCNs from the Services to support monitoring the shipping status should be undertaken for high-visibility shipments, particularly where there are multiple shipments and when cargo is shipped incrementally.

C11. CHAPTER 11

FINANCIAL MANAGEMENT OF DRAWDOWNS

C11.1. FINANCIAL MANAGEMENT OF DRAWDOWNS

The key consideration in financial management of drawdowns is that DoD is not authorized to exceed the drawdown authority provided in the authorizing legislation and the Presidential Determination. (An Anti-Deficiency Act violation would result.) All efforts must be directed toward ensuring that all associated values are identified and tracked.

C11.2. VALUATION OF DRAWDOWN ARTICLES AND SERVICES

C11.2.1. Value of drawdown equipment articles is based on pricing policy contained in the DoD FMR 7000.14R, Volume 15, Chapter 7.

C11.2.1.1. Value of Defense Working Capital Fund (DWCF) items must equate to the DWCF standard price. Note that all DWCF items issued from inventory require funding by the MILDEP processing the requisition (FMR Vol. 12 Chapter 23, Section 2305).

C11.2.1.2. Value of non-excess investment assets not to be replaced, must equate to the sum of (a) the most recent actual procurement cost, (b) modifications or improvements incorporated after production and (c) non-recurring charge if applicable, adjusted for age or condition plus pro rate overhaul cost.

C11.2.1.3. Value of non-excess investment assets to be replaced (DoD budget/FYDP must reflect intent to acquire asset) must equate to the sum of (a) the estimated cost of the replacement and (b) non-recurring charge if applicable, adjusted for age or condition.

C11.2.2. Value of drawdown Military Education and Training shall be based on additional costs that are incurred by the USG in furnishing the training (i.e., FMF Grant/Incremental rate as specified in the DoD FMR Vol. 15).

C11.2.3. Value of services is based on actual costs to the USG for providing the service. Costs include funded portion of civilian salaries, but excludes salaries of the members of the US Armed Forces and unfunded civilian retirement and other benefits.

C11.2.4. FMS Administrative and Contract Administrative Services surcharges are not included in valuation of equipment and services for drawdowns. The valuation of drawdowns of defense articles and services, including military education and training transferred from DoD resources based on special legislation shall be determined on a case by case basis in accordance with the legislation. FMS surcharges are not included in valuation of these special drawdowns.

C11.2.5. Due to the often-abbreviated timelines available to develop V&A data for drawdowns, it is critical to ensure that projected values are as accurate as possible. Because of the short response time, there is a tendency for the Services to inflate their cost estimates until the scope of requirements is clearly defined. There may be subsequent criticism when actual costs are reconciled and found to be lower. However, the important point to remember is that by law DoD may not exceed the authorized authority. The key is close coordination between DSCA and the Service Action Officer's, as the drawdown is executed to reconcile actual vs. projected costs as early as possible.

C11.3. <u>FINANCIAL TRACKING OF DRAWDOWN COSTS</u>

To keep track of projected and actual drawdown values the DSCA OPS-ADMIN and Service Action Officer's keep compatible drawdown spreadsheets so that data can be compared and exchanged in a format that permits easy reconciliation of costs. A sample format is in Appendix 5.

C11.3.1. <u>Minimum Drawdown Tracking Data</u>. To support drawdown financial tracking, the required tracking data is as follows: Item/Service, Quantity, Unit Value (drawdown value), Equipment (Total Quantity Value), Services/Repair, Training (if applicable), Spare Parts, Support Equipment, PC&H, Transport, and Total Item/Service Value (sum of all other categories for each items). Salaries for civilian services should be separately identified. At the DSCA level, this spreadsheet should be organized to permit computation of the overall drawdown value by each category and by each Service/Defense Agency contribution. The sample at Appendix 5 provides such a structure with automatically computed Service/Defense Agency totals.

C11.3.2. <u>O&M Impact - End Items vs. Services/Support Costs</u>. A critical Service consideration for all drawdowns is how much of the projected value reflects actual outlay of current year O&M funds. All of the above categories EXCEPT the Equipment category involve the actual expenditure of Service O&M funds. As a minimum, there will always be O&M outlays to fund PC&H and transportation. If repair services, training, spare parts and support equipment are also required for the drawdown, these categories will usually involve direct O&M expenditures. The Equipment category is not considered to have an O&M impact (except for DWCF materials covered in paragraph C11.4.3) as the equipment was previously purchased and is a "sunk" value to the respective Service. While not having an O&M impact, accurate assessment of a "drawdown" value for equipment items is critical, as equipment frequently constitutes the majority of the value of any given drawdown. Drawdowns that are exclusively services, such as transport services, will have 100% O&M impact.

C11.3.3. <u>Projected versus Actual Costs</u>. Actual value assessments are normally not available until 30-90 days after actual delivery of the equipment. DSCA and Service Action Officer's should maintain close coordination to update and replace projected costs in each category as soon as the firm value can be identified.

C11.4. REIMBURSEMENT FOR PROVIDED DWCF MATERIAL AND SERVICES

One of the contentious Service issues is the OSD Comptroller's policy (DoD FMR Vol. 12, Chapter 23, Section 2305) that requires the Services use O&M funds to reimburse all equipment, materials, or services provided from Defense Working Capital Fund (DWCF) activities, including DLA and USTRANSCOM. The most common items are DLA-managed clothing items, individual equipment, spare parts, tools, and fuel, and support items such as batteries. The Services are required to provide funded (fill/kill) requisitions to DLA for such items. This is NOT considered a "new" procurement as it involves an internal transfer of funds within DoD to provide items that DoD previously purchased and put in its stocks.

C11.5. SERVICE REPORTING OF DRAWDOWN EXECUTION

The formal channel for Service/Defense Agency reporting of drawdown expenditures is the DSCA 1000 System. The DSCA 1000 System is the information management system for tracking, maintaining and aggregating drawdown data to fulfill management information needs and meet legislative reporting requirements. At least monthly, each Service or Agency must enter the appropriate programming and delivery data against appropriate RCNs into the DSCA 1000 System. Data entry has been one of the weakest links in drawdown financial management, as there seems to be a lack of understanding of the importance of timely data entry and a lack of internal Service guidance as to which Service Component (s) should enter and update this data. Therefore, close coordination is essential.

C11.5.1. Entering execution Data. As part of the initial EXORD, the DSCA CPD, with DSCA OPS-ADMIN coordination, assigns Record Control Numbers (RCNs) to each Service or Agency tasked to provide equipment or services for that drawdown. The RCN is a four-position alpha/numeric code assigned to each record in the DSCA 1000 System for identification purposes (see C8.12 Assignment of RCNs). The MAP Element Code field, record positions 47-50, should contain the 4-digit PD number assigned to the drawdown. Record Position 35 always contains "C". Drawdown transactions, including any training related to those drawdowns, will be reported in accordance with Appendix 8.

C11.5.1.1. Each Service/Agency SHOULD immediately enter the PROJECTED value data for each type of equipment or service, it is programmed to provide. As actual value data is received, the PROJECTED value data should be updated with ACTUAL value data in the DSCA 1000 System. See table C11.T1 for input data fields. Appendix 8 provides instructions for input data.

Table C11.T1. Drawdown Transaction

Field Names	Description	Position	Format	Length
CC	Country Name	001-002	Char (alpha?)	2
PY	Program Year	003-006	Char (alpha?)	4
IA	Implementing Agency	007	Char (alpha?)	1
MALC	MILDEP country location	008-017	number	10
BLANK	Blank	018-027	number	10

MFVAL	MILDEP country funded value	028-037		10
MDAT	MILDEP as of date	038-045	YYYYMMDD	8

C11.5.2. <u>United Nations Participation Act (UNPA) Transactions</u>. UN requests for assistance under Section 7 of the UNPA are handled like drawdowns and tracked in the DSCA 1000 System. However, UNPA requests are unique in that they are not reimbursable (unlike Section 607, FAA, transactions) and may involve procurement (unlike drawdowns which are "fill or kill"). To track these transactions and also distinguish them from DoD drawdowns, use the standard United Nations "T9" country code and the 4-digit MAP Element Code (PD number) in record position 47-50, which contains the Tracking Number assigned to the UN request, consisting of three numeric digits and one alpha character in the fourth position of "U" (i.e., XXXU) -the fourth position must always be "U".

C11.5.3. <u>Excess Defense Articles (EDA)</u>. Any EDA items provided in a drawdown should be entered in the DSCA 1000 System with a "Type of Assistance Code" of "C" in record position 35 along with a Source of Supply Code of "E" in record position 65. The "E" Source of Supply code indicates that the item is excess and automatically allows the cost field to remain blank. EDA items provided by drawdown must follow the procedures outlined in Chapter 11 of the SAMM.

C11.6. <u>DRAWDOWN OF FUNDS</u>

C11.6.1. A recent new development has been the drawdown of funds instead of items and services. A drawdown of funds is not specifically addressed in the SAMM, but is handled similarly to a SAMM C11.3 Counter-narcotics assistance-National Defense Authorization Acts, Sections 1004 and 1033.

C11.6.2. An S9 pseudo case designator is used to track the sale of defense articles and/or services to the recipient. The Pseudo LOA itemizes the defense articles and/or services, it is NOT signed by the country and/or organization receiving the articles and/or services.

C11.6.3. A drawdown EXORD is written which breaks out how much funding each Military Department (MILDEP) provides, and what that funding is to be used for. The S9 cases align the funds according to the EXORD.

C11.6.4. Since the MILDEP funding used is Operations and Maintenance (O&M) appropriated funding, it is one-year money. This means that obligations can only be made against the S9 case until the end of the FY the funds are appropriated in. There is a further five years for obligation adjustments and disbursements. At the end of that year, the funds are cancelled. This calls for stringent management of the case to ensure the funds are appropriately handled.

C11.6.5. The O&M funds appropriation is cancelled at the end of the sixth year. Therefore, every effort must be made to have all bills paid and the cases closed before the end of the sixth year.

C11.6.6. A separate holding account should be established for each year that drawdown funds are used on S9 cases. This allows funds from cases that close with funds remaining to be used for cases that close with a need for additional funds. A new EXORD will be required to move the funds through the holding account to the new cases. Appendix 9 provides a chart with a brief synopsis of the Presidential Determined drawdown, flow of funds for an S9 case.

C11.7. CONGRESSIONAL REPORTING

The DSCA OPS-ADMIN Office has the lead for preparing statutorily required reports (also see C12.3 Congressional Reporting).

C12. CHAPTER 12

RECONCILIATION AND REPORTING TO CONGRESS

C12.1. FINANCIAL RECONCILIATION

Immediately after or concurrent with delivery, of the equipment and/or services, the DSCA CPD should coordinate with the Service/Defense Agency Action Officer's to reconcile projected and actual execution value. This effort cannot wait until completion of all deliveries, but should be a continual process as actual values become available. Due to delayed or non-reporting of the data into the DSCA 1000 System by the Service Components, this effort is frequently conducted by exchange/comparison of DSCA and Service Action Officer spreadsheets, and DSCA's 1000 System Report (See appendix 8). Once the CPD determines that all commodities/services actions are completed and/or the drawdown authority is exhausted, the CPD will send out a drawdown termination message, terminating all new supply actions. The closure action allows J4-SILD to close the project code assigned to the drawdown. The termination message will also request Services to report all financial data into the DSCA 1000 System to allow the DSCA OPS-ADMIN Office to prepare its report to Congress.

C12.2. CONGRESSIONAL REPORTING

The DSCA OPS-ADMIN Office has the lead for preparing statutorily required reports.

C12.2.1. FAA, Section 506 Report. FAA, section 506 (reference (b)) requires the Department of Defense (DSCA) to report to Congress details on all the defense articles, defense services, and military education and training delivered to the recipient country or international organization upon delivery or completion of such articles, services, or education and training. The report must also include whether any savings were realized by utilizing commercial transportation services rather than acquiring those services from USG transport assets.

C12.2.2. Special Authorities. For "special" drawdown authorities, there may be additional reporting requirements authorized by legislation in any fiscal year.

C12.2.3. FAA, Section 655. Annual military assistance reporting is required on ALL drawdowns. The report covers defense articles (including excess defense articles (EDA)), defense services, and military training and education furnished by grant under any authority of law, except under title V of the National Security Act of 1947.

C12.2.4. FAA, Section 506. require that the Drug Interdiction and Counter Drug Activities Report be reported to Congress listing equipment DoD provided via counternarcotics drawdown efforts and the DoD's plans for replacing it, whether totally, partially, or not at all. This report gives Congress a sense of the adverse impact of drawdowns on DoD resources and US military readiness. In addition to equipment listings, DSCA requests the Services to also provide impact statements for submission to Congress.

(Intentionally Left Blank)

APPENDIX 1

AP1. APPENDIX 1
Drawdown List 1963- 2004

FY	PD No.	Country or Region	Authority	Purpose	FY Total ($ millions)
1963	PD63-15	India	506(a)(1)	War With China	$55.0
1965	PD65-12	MAP/Vietnam	506(a)(1)	Military Assistance	$75.0
1966	PD66-06	MAP/Vietnam	506(a)(1)	Military Assistance	$300.0
1974	PD74-12/-19	Cambodia	506(a)(1)	Military Assistance	$250.0
1975	PD75-09	Cambodia	506(a)(1)	N. Vietnamese Threat	$75.0
1980	PD80-21	Thailand	506(a)(1)	N. Vietnamese Threat	$1.1
1981	PD81-00	Liberia	506(a)(1)	Support Coup	$3.4
1981	PD81-02/-04	El Salvador	506(a)(1)	Guerrilla Threat	$25.0
1982	PD82-05	El Salvador	506(a)(1)	Guerrilla Threat	$55.0
1983	PD83-08/-09	Chad	506(a)(1)	War With Libya	$25.0
1986	PD86-06	Chad	506(a)(1)	War With Libya	$10.0
1986	PD86-08	Honduras	506(a)(1)	Threat from Nicaragua	$20.0
1986	PD86-13	Philippines	506(a)(1)	Earthquake	$10.0
1987	PD87-05/-13	Chad	506(a)(1)	War With Libya	$25.0
1988	PD	Afghan/Pakistan	552(c)(2)	UN Observer Group-DoD Transport	$0.22
1989	PD89-06	Jamaica	506(a)(1)	Hurricane	$10.0
1989	PD89-24	Colombia	506(a)(1)	Counternarcotics	$65.0
1990	PD90-33	Counternarcotics	506(a)(2)	Counternarcotics	$53.3
1990	PD90-40	Israel	506(a)(1)	Desert Storm	$74.0
1990	PD90-41	Philippines	506(a)(2)	Mt. Pinatubo Eruption	$10.0
1991	PD91-01	Israel	506(a)(1)	Desert Storm	$43.0
1991	PD91-16	Turkey	506(a)(1)	Desert Storm	$32.0
1991	PD91-26	Turkey	506(a)(2)	Kurdish relief	$25.0
1991	PD91-31	Turkey	506(a)(2)	Kurdish relief	$50.0

APPENDIX 1

FY	PD No.	Country or Region	Authority	Purpose	FY Total ($ millions)
1991	PD91-35	Bangladesh	506(a)(2)	Cyclone	$20.0
1992	PD92-05	Senegal	552(c)(2)	Support Deployment to Liberia	$10.0
1992	PD92-17	Mexico	506(a)(2)	Counternarcotics	$26.0
1992	PD92-23	Israel	599B	Special Authority	$47.0
1992	PD92-48	Colombia	506(a)(2)	Counternarcotics	$7.0
1992	PD92-49	Pakistan	506(a)(2)	Flood	$5.0
1993	PD93-17	Israel	599B	Special Authority	$491.1
1993	PD93-27	Ecuador	506(a)(2)	Disaster Relief	$2.0
1993	PD93-43	UN	552(c)(2)	Somalia Peacekeeping efforts	$25.0
1993	PD93-45	LAction Officers	575AC	POW/MIA	$11.8
1993	PD93-99	UNK		UNK	$3.9
1994	PD94-	UN	1511(103-1)	Serbia Border Sanctions Enforcement	$5.6
1994	PD94-07	Egypt	552(c)(2)	Return of M113 A2's to EG	$13.5
1994	PD94-20	Israel	559B	Special Authority	$161.9
1994	PD94-21	Israel	552(c)(2)	Palestine Police	$4.0
1994	PD94-34	Dominican Republic	506(a)(1)	Anti-Smuggle Assistance	$15.0
1994	PD94-41	Jamaica	506(a)(1)	Haiti Refugee Assistance	$1.5
1994	PD94-44	Rwanda T9	552(a)(2)	Disaster Relief/Refugee care	$75.0
1994	PD94-50	Haiti	506(a)(1)	Mult-nat. Coalition Force	$50.0
1995	PD95-03	Israel	559B	Special Authority	$75.0
1995	PD95-17	Israel (Palestine Police)	552(c)(2)	Peacekeeping	$5.0
1995	PD95-28	Haiti	552(c)(2)	Peacekeeping	$5.0
1995	PD95-29	Bosnia, UK, FR	506(a)(1)	Rapid Reaction Force Transportation	$12.0
1995	PD95-33	Bosnia, UK, FR	506(a)(1)	Rapid Reaction Force Communication Equip	$3.0
1995	PD95-34	Bosnia, UK, FR	506(a)(1)	Rapid Reaction Force	$17.0

FY	PD No.	Country or Region	Authority	Purpose	FY Total ($ millions)
1996	PD96-11	Jordan	sec 572	Special authority	$100.0
1996	PD96-17	Israel (Never executed)	506(a)(1) and 552	Explosive detection disarming (DoD portion)	$22.0
1996	PD96-39	Bosnia	sec 540	Special Authority	$100.0
1996	PD96-42	Vietnam	sec 535	POW/MIA	$3.0
1996	PD96-50	Cambodia	sec 535	POW/MIA	$0.2
1996	PD96-52	Haiti	552(c)(2)	Training of HNP	$1.0
1996	PD96-53	Africa ER, ET, UG	506(a)(1)	Sudan Containment	$10.0
1996	PD96-55	Africa LI, Mali, IV	506(a)(1)	ECOMOG	$5.0
1996	PD96-56	Africa LI, Mali, IV	552(c)(2)	ECOMOG	$10.0
1996	PD96-57	L.America/Carib RSS	506(a)(2)	Counternarcotics	$75.0
1997	PD97-09	Mexico	506(a)(2)	Counternarcotics	$37.0
1997	PD97-12	Turcoman Monitor	552(c)(2)	Peacekeeping	$4.0
1997	PD97-14	Iraqi Refugees	506(a)(2)	Operation Pacific Heaven	$10.0
1997	PD97-38	L.America/Carib RSS	506(a)(2)	Counternarcotics	$20.0
1998	PD98-19	(ME) Jordan	SEC 572	Special Authority	$25.0
1998	PD98-41	L.America/Carib RSS	506(a)(2)	Counternarcotics	$70.0
1999	PD99-03	L. America: HO, NU, ES, GT	506(a)(2)	Emergency Disaster opns	$30.0
1999	PD99-04	L. America: HO, NU, ES, GT	506(a)(2)	Emergency Disaster opns	$45.0
1999	PD99-18	Jordan	FY99 Ops Act	Special Authority	$25.0
1999	PD99-20	Kosovo Refugees	552(c)(2)	Peacekeeping	$25.0
1999	PD99-32	Tunisia	FY99/ops Act	Special authority	$5.0
1999	PD99-34	Africa, NI, GH, SL, Mali, GV	506(a)(1)	ECOMOG	$3.0
1999	PD99-35	Kosovo war crimes YU	99 For Ops Act	FBI- Intlo war crimes tribunal YU	$5.0
1999	PD99-39	East Timor, Indonesia	506(a)(1)	Multi Forces Intl Ops	$55.0
1999	PD99-40	Kosovo-Protection Corps	552(c)(2)	UN mission to develop KP Corp	$5.0
1999	PD99-43	L.America, CO, PE, EC, PN	506(a)(2)	Counternarcotics	$69.7
2000	PD00-05	Iraqi Liberation Act (ME)	PL105-338	Trng 4 students at Hulburt Field, FL ($16K)	$5.0

APPENDIX 1

FY	PD No.	Country or Region	Authority	Purpose	FY Total ($ millions)
2000	PD00-09	Venezuela	506(a)(2)	Emergency Disaster opns	$20.0
2000	PD00-17	(ASA) Africa SF, BC, MZ, ZI, ZA, MA	506(a)(2)	Emergency Disaster opns	$37.6
2000	PD00-27	Sierra Leone	506(a)(1)	Military Assistance to UNAMSIL and other countries involved in peacekeeping effort	$18.0
2000	PD00-33	Tunisia	PL106-113	EDA and PCH&T	$4.0
2001	PD01-04	Sierra Leone	506(a)(1)	Military Assistance to UNAMSIL and other countries involved in peacekeeping effort	$36.0
2001	PD01-24	Tunisia	PL106-429	EDA C-130B spare parts and PCH&T	$5.0
2001	PD02-16	Nigeria	506(a)(1)	Military Assistance to Sierra Leone	$4.0
2002	PD02-17	Georgia	505	Georgia Military Training and Equipment	$4.0
2002	PD02-18	Afghanistan	506(a)(1)	Emergency Military Assistance to Afghanistan	$2.0
2002	PD02-20	Georgia	506(a)(1	Georgia Military Training and Equipment	$21.0
2002	PD02-24	Philippines	506(a)(1	Immediate Military assistance counterterrorism	$10.0
2002	PD02-28	Tunisia	PL107-115	EDA C-130B spare parts and PCH&T	$5.0
2003	PD03-06	Iraq	PL106-429	Iraq Liberation	$92.0
2003	PD03-15	Afghanistan	PL107-327	Military Education and Training	$165.0
2004	PD04-15	Afghanistan	PL107-327	Transportation Resources, Defense Articles, Services and Training	$135.0

APPENDIX 1

APPENDIX 2

AP2. <u>APPENDIX 2</u>

COMPTROLLER OF THE DEPARTMENT OF DEFENSE

WASHINGTON, DC 20301-1100

July 28, 1994

MEMORANDUM FOR ASSISTANT SECRETARY OF THE ARMY (FINANCIAL
MANAGEMENT)
ASSISTANT SECRETARY OF THE NAVY (FINANCIAL
MANAGEMENT)
ASSISTANT SECRETARY OF THE AIR FORCE (FINANCIAL
MANAGEMENT AND COMPTROLLER)
COMPTROLLER, DEFENSE LOGISTICS AGENCY
COMPTROLLER, UNITED STATES TRANSPORTATION
COMMAND
DIRECTOR, FORCE STRUCTURE, RESOURCES AND
ASSESMENT, THE JOINT STAFF

SUBJECT: Reimbursement of DBOF Activities for Contingency Operations and
Humanitarian Efforts

This memorandum provides policy for funding contingency operations costs at DBOF activities and documents the funding procedures for contingencies and similar actions that have normally been followed in the past. The intent is to clarify the process and establish Military Department responsibilities for payment. This policy will be incorporated into various instructions as they are revised and published.

All DBOF business areas, including transportation services provided by USTRANSCOM, operate on a reimbursement basis with users paying for goods and services provided. Payment for contingency operations, including deployment or other emergency response for military or humanitarian assistance, is no exception: The users ordering the DBOF service must pay the bill, and no orders are to be accepted without funding. The Military Department Headquarters is responsible for determining which level within the Military Department will pay (ie.... Unit, major command, or Military Department level). This process also applies when a Unified Commander tasks a Service-funded unit to perform a mission (such as transportation of Service personnel or equipment by USTRANSCOM). The parent Military Department that owns the equipment or personnel is responsible for payment of costs incurred to accomplish the mission.

The sole exception to this policy occurs when CINCTRANSCOM receives an order from JCS requiring transportation of non-U.S. owned equipment and/or non-U.S. personnel such as unreimbursed efforts in support of the U.N. In these instances, Army will pay MTMC costs, Navy will pay MSC costs, and Air Force will pay AMC costs.

Bills can be centralized for more convenient processing if appropriate; however, billings will be forwarded to the appropriate Military Department within 30 days from commencement of the contingency operation or humanitarian effort. Payment of these bills, including transportation bills, by the Military Departments must be made in a timely manner.

This guidance does not address any contingency operation designated by the Secretary of Defense as a "National Contingency Operation" under the Provision of 10 U.S.C. Section 127. Special rules would apply for such an operation, and those rules would be promulgated separately in conjunction with any designation by the Secretary under the provisions of that section.

//SIGNED//

Alice C. Maroni
Principal Deputy Comptroller

APPENDIX 3

AP3. APPENDIX 3

DRAWDOWN PLANNING/DEVELOPMENT

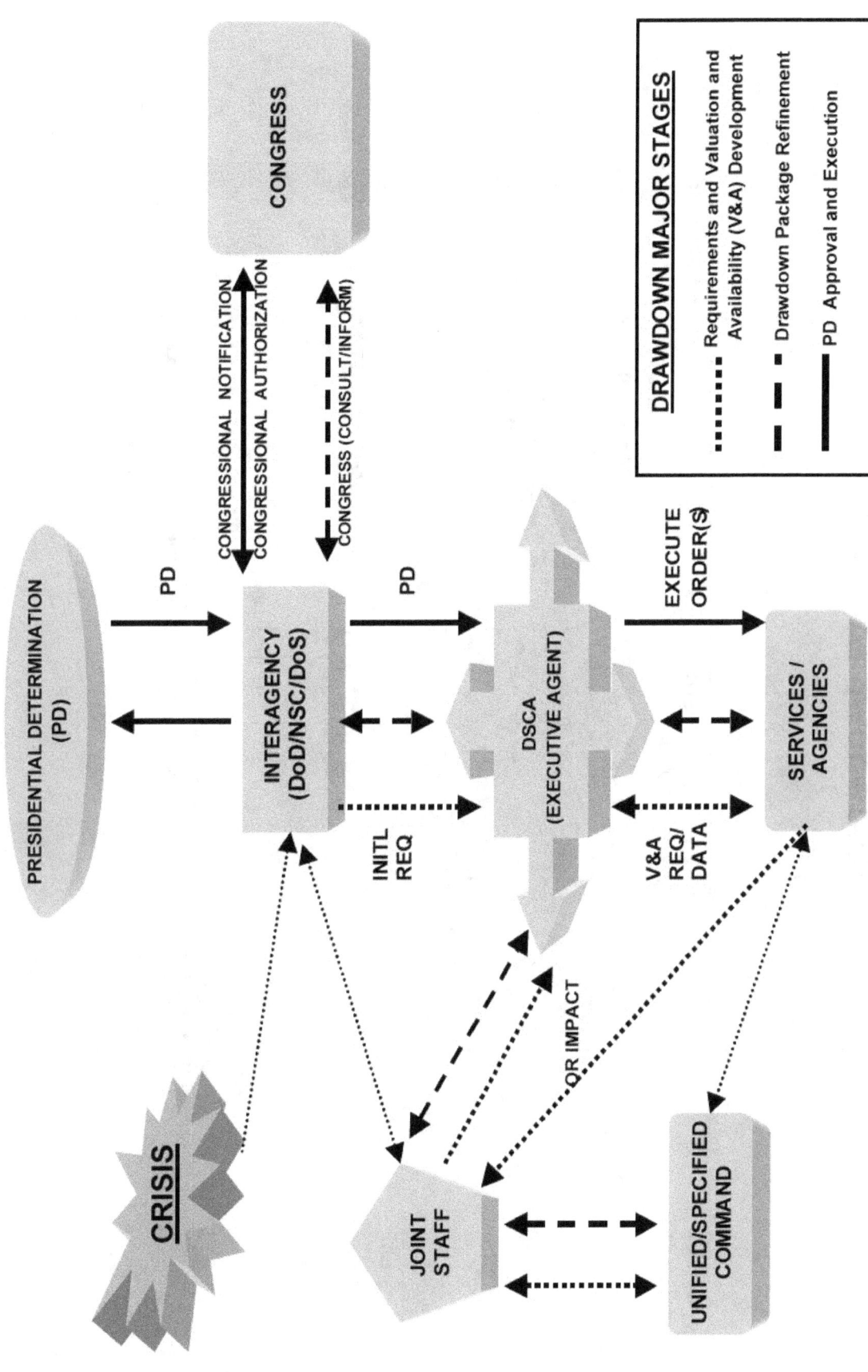

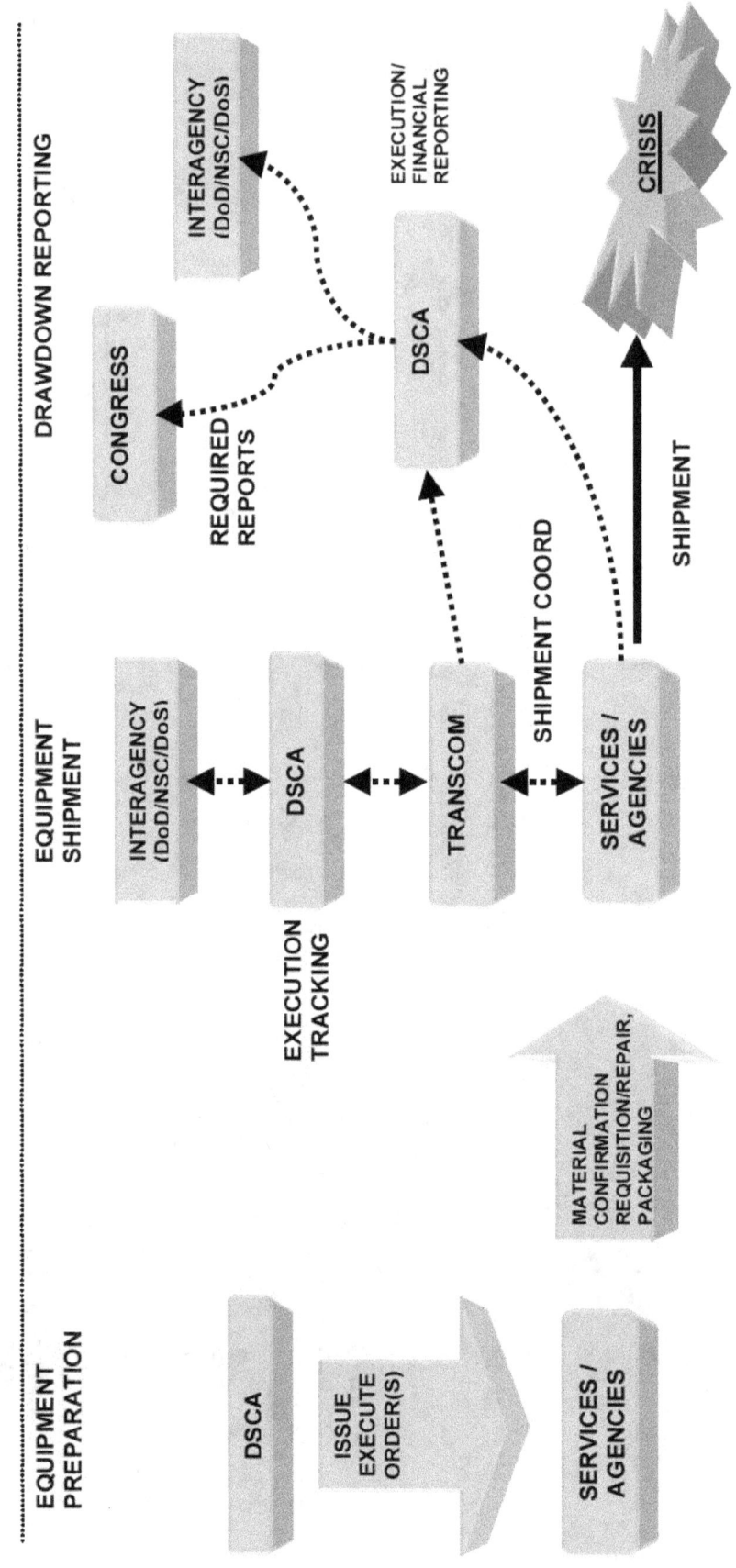

Drawdown Execution

APPENDIX 4

AP4. APPENDIX 4
SAMPLE PRESIDENTIAL DETERMINATION (PD) AND MEMORANDUM OF JUSTIFICATION

THE WHITE HOUSE

WASHINGTON

September 30, 1999

99 OCT -1 AM 11: 38

Presidential Determination
No. __99-43__

MEMORANDUM FOR THE SECRETARY OF STATE
                THE SECRETARY OF THE TREASURY
                THE SECRETARY OF DEFENSE
                THE ATTORNEY GENERAL
                THE SECRETARY OF TRANSPORTATION

SUBJECT: Drawdown Under Section 506(a)(2) of the Foreign
                Assistance Act to Provide Counter-Drug Assistance
                to Colombia, Peru, Ecuador, and Panama

Pursuant to the authority vested in me by section 506(a)(2)
of the Foreign Assistance Act of 1961, as amended, 22 U.S.C.
2318(a)(2) (the "Act"), I hereby determine that it is in the
national interest of the United States to draw down articles
and services from the inventory and resources of the Department
of Defense, military education and training from the Department
of Defense, and articles and services from the inventory and
resources of the Departments of Justice, State, Transportation,
and the Treasury for the purpose of providing international
anti-narcotics assistance to Colombia, Peru, Ecuador, and
Panama.

Therefore, I direct the drawdown of up to $72.55 million of
articles and services from the inventory and resources of the
Departments of Defense, Transportation, Justice, State, and
the Treasury, and military education and training from the
Department of Defense, for Colombia, Peru, Ecuador, and Panama
for the purposes and under the authorities of chapter 8 of
part I of the Act.

As a matter of policy and consistent with past practice, my
Administration will seek to ensure that the assistance furnished
under this drawdown is not provided to any unit of any foreign
country's security forces if that unit is credibly alleged to
have committed gross violations of human rights unless the
government of such country is taking effective measures to bring
the responsible members of that unit to justice.

I-99/013034
100812 /99

MEMORANDUM OF JUSTIFICATION
FOR USE OF SECTION 506(a) (2) AUTHORITY
TO DRAW DOWN ARTICLES, SERVICES, AND MILITARY
EDUCATION AND TRAINING

Due primarily to the rapidly deteriorating situation in Colombia, there is a critical need for us to provide additional Counternarcotics (CN) support to the governments of Colombia, Peru, Ecuador, and Panama. Increased efforts by these governments to eradicate illegal drug crops produced in their countries and to interdict drugs en route through their countries at once reduce the availability of drug-financed support to anti-government forces in these countries and to reduce the flow of drugs into the United States. Specifically, these governments are in critical need of counternarcotics (CN) assistance beyond that which we can provide through International Narcotics Control (INC) funding. We propose that such assistance be provided under the authority of section 506 (a) (2) of the FAA.

Under our proposal, the President would direct a drawdown of up to $69.7 million in articles, services, transportation, and military education and training from the Department of Defense to support our counternarcotics strategy within the Western Hemisphere. Of this, we estimate that approximately $56 million would be used to bolster the counternarcotics efforts of the Colombian National Police (CNP) and Colombian military elements which directly support the CN effort; approximately $4.0 million would go to support the Peruvian National Police and elements of the Peruvian military; approximately $3.4 million would support police and military elements in Ecuador, and approximately $0.3 million would support security forces in Panama. Finally, approximately $6.0 million of this authority would be expended from DoD operational funds for packing, crating, handling, transportation, and related support for this package.

The President would also direct a drawdown of up to $1.1 million in articles and services from the Department of Transportation Coast Guard (USCG) to support counternarcotics efforts in Colombia. (This authority will be used to facilitate hot handoff of Coast Guard vessels we intend to provide to Colombia, as Excess Defense Articles (EDA) early in FY Ol. It will not affect the current EDA allocation program.)

1

The President would also direct a drawdown of up to $625 thousand in articles and services from the Department of the Treasury to support counternarcotics efforts. Of this, we would estimate that approximately $525 thousand would support Ecuador and the remainder would support Panama.

The President would also direct a drawdown of up to $125 thousand in articles and services from the Department of Justice (DEA) to support counternarcotics efforts. Of this, we would estimate that approximately $50 thousand would support Panama and approximately $75 thousand would support Ecuador.

Finally, the President would direct a drawdown of approximately $1.0 million in articles and services from the Department of State (INL) to support counternarcotics efforts in Colombia.

The Director of the Office of National Drug Control Policy (ONDCP), the NSC staff, the Secretaries of Defense, Transportation, and the Treasury, and the Attorney General concur with this proposal.

Depending on the situation in receiving countries, selected end items provided will be accompanied by a package of available spare parts, equipment reception assistance, and user and maintenance training as appropriate--and as availability from agency inventory and resources dictate.

The narcotics and security situation in Colombia continues to deteriorate. Coca cultivation, including higher yield varieties, has increased close to 50 percent over the last two years. Heroin cultivation and production has also increased. The vast majority of the new coca cultivation is in Putumayo and Caqueta--areas where the GOC has not been able to conduct effective CN operations due to infestation by heavily armed anti-government forces supporting trafficking interests. Complicating the GOC's ability to meet these challenges, the Colombian economy is in the worst condition that it has seen in 50 years. The approximately $58.1 million in this package would support the Colombian Military and National Police in their effort to conduct vigorous CN operations throughout the country-but concentrating in the South. We would also increase the Colombian Air Force's ability to interdict air trafficking into, out of, and within Colombia-and onward toward the United States. Support for the CNP will facilitate its law enforcement, interdiction, and eradication programs-and its ability to conduct joint CN operations with the Colombian Military.

UNCLASSIFIED

2

We anticipate providing the CNP with weapons, ammunition, explosives, spare parts, field and flight gear, operational fuel, field aviation support equipment, base defensive items, and training. For the Colombian military, we anticipate providing aircraft spares, fuel, weapons, ammunition, explosives, field and flight gear, hot handoff of USCG coastal patrol craft to be provided under Excess Defense Article authority, base defensive items, field rations, aviation management support, and training.

The effect of this situation is not limited to Colombia. In Peru, despite intensive efforts by CN forces, traffickers are adjusting to the GOP's highly successful operation against air trafficking. Not only are they adjusting their flight patterns, but also cocaine base is reported to be moving on Peruvian rivers and overland across the Andes--where some of it was processed into HCl for subsequent shipment from Peruvian ports and airports. We intend to provide some $4.0 million of assistance to furnish the Peruvian National Police, Air Force, and Coast Guard with aircraft spares, field and flight equipment, field rations, life support equipment, field aviation support equipment, fuel, training, and field bridging equipment.

Ecuador continues to be a major transit country for cocaine hydrochloride (HCI), primary from Colombia, destined for the United States and Europe. Colombian traffickers control much of the cocaine smuggled into Ecuador. Colombian heroin and Peruvian HCI also transit Ecuador. Ecuador is used to import essential chemicals for cocaine production and to launder money. The Government of Ecuador (GOE) fully cooperates with the USG in the fight against narcotics trafficking. We anticipate furnishing approximately $4.0 million of assistance to the Ecuadorian Military and Police-particularly those serving in or supporting units along the frontier with Colombia. We plan to provide them with spare parts, weapons, ammunition, and training.

Panama's role as a major transit point for illicit drugs heading to North America and other global markets is enhanced by its proximity to Colombia, remoteness of its frontier with that country, location on key transportation routes, openness to trade, and generally weak controls along borders and coasts. We must continue to improve the CN capabilities of Panama's weak security forces-including ground-based CN units, the National Maritime Service (SNM-coast guard), and National Air Service (SAN)--enabling them to become effective participants in efforts to intercept illicit drug shipments. With some $450 thousand of assistance we would like to provide Panama with small boats, counternarcotics equipment, patrol and administrative vehicles, weapons, night vision devices, crew safety items, support equipment, and training.

UNCLASSIFIED

3

As mentioned earlier, DoD will furnish packing, crating, handling, transportation, and related support for this package valued at approximately $6.0 million of drawdown authority.

Section 506(a) (2) Drawdown

No assistance will actually be delivered under the drawdown unless the particular recipient government has provided appropriate end-use, retransfer, and security assurances in accordance with section 505 of the FAA, including agreement that equipment provided under this drawdown will be used for counternarcotics purposes.

The President has determined that the provision of the aid described herein is in the national interest of the United States. The drawdown will be directed during fiscal year 1999, with the result that it would count against the ceilings for fiscal year 1999, though it is anticipated that deliveries would be completed thereafter.

UNCLASSIFIED
4

APPENDIX 5

AP5. APPENDIX 5
(PD 99-43 506(a)(2) Counternarcotics Delivery Report)

Customer	Supplier	Line item	Item	Qty	Exord value	Shipments value	Delta	RCN	Delivery status	Shipping notes
BARBADOS RSS										
	USAF	4.08.01	FLT EQP SETS: FLT SUITS, GLOVES & BOOTS	6	$10,000.00	$2,353.00	$7,647.00	CB01	COMPLETE	COMPLETE: 9 REQUISITONS SHIPPED. REPORT FROM RSS MLGRP 02/2000 3EA 42S COVERALLS LOST.
	USAF	4.08.02	C-26 A/B AIRCRAFT	2	$6,000,000.00	$2,001,062.00	$3,998,938.00	CB00	COMPLETE	COMPLETE: 1ST A/C DEL JAN 99. 2ND DELIVERED TO DOS MAY 99. 02/2000 REPORT FROM RSS MLGRP 1EA A/C IN COUNTRY. OTHER STILL AT DOS FACILITY ONGOING MODIFICATIONS.
	USAF	4.08.02F	C-26 A/B AIRCRAFT FERRY	1	$20,000.00	$20,985.00	($985.00)	CB17	COMPLETE	COMPLETE: JAN 99 AND MAY 1999. 02/2000 REPORT FROM RSS MLGRP 1EA A/C IN COUNTRY. OTHER STILL AT DOS FACILITY ONGOING MODIFICATIONS.
	USAF	PC&HBBUSAF	PC&H CHARGES USAF	1	$0.00	$0.00	$0.00	CB18	COMPLETE	
	USAF	TRANSBBUSAF	TRANSPORTATION CHARGES USAF	1	$235.00	$235.00	$0.00	CB19	COMPLETE	
					Sum Of exord value: $6,030,235.00	Sum Of shipments value: $2,024,635.00	Sum Of delta: $4,005,600.00			
COLOMBIA AF										
	USA	1.09.12	UH-1H HULKS FOR SPARES	20	$3,000,000.00	$170,060.00	$2,829,940.00	CC40	COMPLETE	COMPLETE: 1 REQUISITION (BCOT0C71049002) SHIPPED. TOTAL COST FOR 20 UH-1HS REPORTED AS $170,060.00. COSTS REFLECT SALVAGE VALUE FOR HULKS.
	USA	1.09.12TECH1	OTHER TECHNICAL ASSISTANCE TEAM	1	$70,000.00	$70,000.00	$0.00	CC41	COMPLETE	COMPLETE: 1 PSEUDO REQUISITION.
	USA	1.09.12TECH2	OTHER TECHNICAL ASSISTANCE TEAM	1	$25,000.00	$25,000.00	$0.00	CC42	COMPLETE	COMPLETE: 1 PSEUDO REQUISITION.
	USA	PC&HCOAFUSA	PC&H CHARGES USA	1	$64,904.00	$64,904.00	$0.00	CC58	COMPLETE	(RCN duplicate)
	USA	TRANSCOAFUSA	TRANSPORTATION CHARGES USA	1	$193,300.00	$40,000.00	$153,300.00	CC59	COMPLETE	Trans costs reser by ODMA (RCN duplicate)
	USAF	1.10.05	UTILITY VEHICLES	15	$869,000.00	$330,891.00	$538,109.00	CA20	COMPLETE	Completed 15 vehicles shipped
	USAF	1.10.06	C-130 SPARES LOT	1	$3,000,000.00	$1,188,295.00	$1,811,705.00	CA21	COMPLETE	Completed 259 requisitions shipped
	USAF	1.10.07	UH-60 SPARES LOT	1	$3,000,000.00	$2,695,056.00	$304,944.00	CA22	COMPLETE	Completed 11 requisitions shipped
	USAF	2.02.02	C-26 A/B AIRCRAFT	3	$9,000,000.00	$3,001,593.00	$5,998,407.00	CA23	COMPLETE	Completed a/c delivered 18 Nov 97
	USAF	2.02.02F	C-26 A/B AIRCRAFT FERRY	1	$30,000.00	$25,233.00	$4,767.00	CA37	COMPLETE	Completed Nov 97
	USAF	PC&HCOAFUSAF	PC&H CHARGES USAF	1	$222,250.00	$222,250.00	$0.00	CA38	COMPLETE	
	USAF	TRANSCOAFUSAF	TRANSPORTATION CHARGES USAF	1	$714,375.00	$714,375.00	$0.00	CA39	COMPLETE	
					Sum Of exord value: $20,188,829.00	Sum Of shipments value: $8,547,657.00	Sum Of delta: $11,641,172.00			
COLOMBIA AR										
	USA	1.09.05	GPS TRIMBLE	45	$0.00	$0.00	$0.00		CANCEL	CANCELED. NOT AVAILABLE FROM INVENTORY.
	USA	1.09.06	LENSATIC COMPASS	500	$0.00	$0.00	$0.00	AA20	CANCEL	REQUISITION BCOA0C7100D001 KILLED/CANCELED. ITEM NOT AVAILABLE FROM INVENTORY.
	USA	1.09.07	FLACK VESTS	600	$0.00	$223,145.00	($223,145.00)	AA21	COMPLETE	4 REQUISITIONS: 3 SHIPPED. 250 LG, 350 MD, AND 500 1ST AID CASES LC1, 1 KILLED/CANCELED.
	USA	1.09.08	BULLET PROOF VESTS	320	$0.00	$0.00	$0.00	AA21	CANCEL	REQUISITION BCOA0C70990026 KILLED/CANCELED. NOT AVAILABLE FROM INVENTORY.
	USA	3.03.17	SECURE MOTOROLA RADIO	45	$0.00	$0.00	$0.00		CANCEL	CANCELED. NOT AVAILABLE FROM INVENTORY.
	USA	3.03.18	SECURE MOTOROLA REPEATER STATIONS	15	$0.00	$0.00	$0.00		CANCEL	CANCELED. NOT AVAILABLE FROM INVENTORY.
	USA	3.03.19	MOTOROLA BATTERY CHARGERS	15	$0.00	$0.00	$0.00		CANCEL	CANCELED. NOT AVAILABLE FROM INVENTORY.
	USA	3.03.20	MOTOROLA RADIO KEYLOADER W/CABLES ADAPTER & CHARGER	1	$0.00	$0.00	$0.00		CANCEL	CANCELED. NOT AVAILABLE FROM INVENTORY.
	USA	TRANSCOARUSA	TRANSPORTATION CHARGES USA	1	$72,543.00	$72,543.00	$0.00	AA39	COMPLETE	2 PSEUDO REQUISITIONS. TRANSPORTATION COSTS RESERVED BY ODMA.
					Sum Of exord value: $72,543.00	Sum Of shipments value: $295,688.00	Sum Of delta: ($223,145.00)			

AP5. APPENDIX 5
(PD 99-43 506(a)(2) Counternarcotics Delivery Report)

Customer	Supplier	Line item	Item	Qty	Exord value	Shipments value	Delta	RCN	Delivery status	Shipping notes
COLOMBIA MC										
	USA	3.03.09	AN/PRC132 HF/VHF SECURE COMMO	10	$0.00	$0.00	$0.00		CANCEL	CANCELED. NOT AVAILABLE FROM INVENTORY.
	USA	3.03.10	SECURE HF MANPACK	20	$0.00	$0.00	$0.00		CANCEL	CANCELED. NOT AVAILABLE FROM INVENTORY.
	USA	3.03.11	SECURE HF BASE STATIONS	20	$0.00	$0.00	$0.00		CANCEL	CANCELED. NOT AVAILABLE FROM INVENTORY.
	USA	3.03.12	SECURE VHF BASE STATIONS	20	$0.00	$0.00	$0.00		CANCEL	CANCELED. NOT AVAILABLE FROM INVENTORY.
	USA	3.03.13	SECURE MOTOROLA RADIOS	45	$0.00	$0.00	$0.00		CANCEL	CANCELED. NOT AVAILABLE FROM INVENTORY.
	USA	3.03.14	SECURE MOTOROLA REPEATER STATIONS	15	$0.00	$0.00	$0.00		CANCEL	CANCELED. NOT AVAILABLE FROM INVENTORY.
	USA	3.03.15	MOTOROLA BATTERY CHARGERS	15	$0.00	$0.00	$0.00		CANCEL	CANCELED. NOT AVAILABLE FROM INVENTORY.
	USA	3.03.16	MOTOROLA RADIO KEYLOADER W/CABLES ADAPTER & CHARGER	1	$0.00	$0.00	$0.00		CANCEL	CANCELED. NOT AVAILABLE FROM INVENTORY.
	USN	2.03.01	MKII PATROL BOATS OR EQUIVALENT	6	$295,000.00	$1,155,000.00	($860,000.00)	BA20	COMPLETE	Boat cost includes $12,500 per boat for rehab done by USN. Unit cost per boat $180,000.00
	USN	2.03.01PCH	PC&H MKII PATROL BOATS OR EQUIVALENT	6	$0.00	$6,000.00	($6,000.00)	BA38	COMPLETE	PC&H for each boat $1,000.00
	USN	2.03.01TRANS	TRANSPORT MKII PATROL BOATS OR EQUIVALENT	6	$0.00	$120,000.00	($120,000.00)	BA39	COMPLETE	Transport cost for each boat $20,000.00
					Sum Of exord value: $295,000.00	Sum Of shipments value: $1,281,000.00	Sum Of delta: ($986,000.00)			
COLOMBIA NP										
	USA	1.09.01	UH-1H	12	$1,800,000.00	$102,036.00	$1,697,964.00	AA00	COMPLETE	1 REQUISITION (BC0E0C71049001) SHIPPED. TOTAL COST FOR 12 UH-1HS REPORTED AS $102,036.00. INL BROUGHT THE A/C INTO B CONDITION BEFORE SHIPMENT.
	USA	1.09.01OTH	UH-1H OTHER TECH ASSISTANCE TEAM	1	$30,000.00	$25,000.00	$5,000.00	AA02	COMPLETE	1 PSEUDO REQUISITION RELATED TO UH-1H TECHNICAL ASSISTANCE TEAM.
	USA	1.09.01QAT	UH-1H QAT USG TEAM IN COUNTRY	1	$30,000.00	$30,000.00	$0.00	AA01	COMPLETE	1 PSEUDO REQUISITION RELATED TO UH-1H DELIVERY TO COLOMBIA
	USA	1.09.02	FLACK VESTS	500	$0.00	$185,350.00	($185,350.00)	AA04	COMPLETE	2 REQUISITIONS SHIPPED, 250 LG, 250 MD.
	USA	1.09.03	FIELD SETS: LBE, CANTEEN PAIR, RUCKSACK & JUNGLE BOOTS LG	2,000	$600,000.00	$269,742.50	$330,257.50	AA04	COMPLETE	51 REQUISITIONS: 23 SHIPPED, 28 KILLED/CANCELED.
	USA	1.09.04	LENSATIC COMPASSES	250	$0.00	$0.00	$0.00	AA05	CANCEL	7 REQUISITIONS KILLED/CANCELED DUE TO NO AVAILABILITY OF STOCK.
	USA	3.03.01	400W AMPLIFIERS	13	$0.00	$0.00	$0.00		CANCEL	CANCELED. NOT AVAILABLE FROM INVENTORY.
	USA	3.03.02	400W ANTENNA TUNERS	13	$0.00	$0.00	$0.00		CANCEL	CANCELED. NOT AVAILABLE FROM INVENTORY.
	USA	3.03.03	MULTIFREQ OMNI CONICAL GAIN-TYPE	13	$0.00	$0.00	$0.00		CANCEL	CANCELED. NOT AVAILABLE FROM INVENTORY.
	USA	3.03.04	GROUNDING SYSTEM (CABLES, WIRES, ETC)	13	$0.00	$0.00	$0.00		CANCEL	CANCELED. NOT AVAILABLE FROM INVENTORY.
	USA	3.03.05	HAND HELD UNITS W/ACCESSORIES	60	$0.00	$0.00	$0.00		CANCEL	CANCELED. NOT AVAILABLE FROM INVENTORY.
	USA	3.03.06	SECURE RADIO KEY LOADERS W/ACCESSORIES	10	$0.00	$0.00	$0.00		CANCEL	CANCELED. NOT AVAILABLE FROM INVENTORY.
	USA	3.03.07	SECURE DVP-XL REPEATERS	6	$0.00	$0.00	$0.00		CANCEL	CANCELED. NOT AVAILABLE FROM INVENTORY.
	USA	3.03.08	12DB GAIN OMNI/ANTENNA FOR DVP-XL	6	$0.00	$0.00	$0.00		CANCEL	CANCELED. NOT AVAILABLE FROM INVENTORY.
	USA	PC&HCONPUSA	PC&H CHARGES USA	1	$63,578.00	$63,473.00	$105.00	AA18	COMPLETE	2 PSEUDO REQUISITIONS.
	USA	TRANSCONPUSA	TRANSPORTATION CHARGES USA	1	$141,880.00	$125,023.00	$16,857.00	AA19	COMPLETE	2 PSEUDO REQUISITIONS. TRANSPORTATION COSTS RESERVED BY ODMA.
	USAF	1.10.01	FLT EQP SETS: HELMETS, FLT SUITS, GLOVES & BOOTS	100	$78,584.00	$77,259.00	$1,325.00	CA00	COMPLETE	Completed: 21 reqs delivered
	USAF	1.10.02	MRE CASES	333	$18,000.00	$25,561.00	($7,561.00)	CA01	COMPLETE	Completed 333 cases shipped
	USAF	1.10.03	5.56MM (A1) BALL AMMO	2,000,000	$420,000.00	$615,065.00	($195,065.00)	CA02	COMPLETE	Completed 1,999,200 rounds shipped
	USAF	1.10.04	JUNGLE BOOTS PAIRS	4,000	$201,015.00	$201,015.00	$0.00	CA03	COMPLETE	Completed 4000 pairs shipped
	USAF	2.02.01	C-26 A/B AIRCRAFT	2	$6,000,000.00	$2,001,062.00	$3,998,938.00	CA04	COMPLETE	Completed a/c delivered 23 Oct 97

AP5. APPENDIX 5

(PD 99-43 506(a)(2) Counternarcotics Delivery Report)

Customer	Supplier	Line item	Item	Qty	Exord value	Shipments value	Delta	RCN	Delivery status	Shipping notes
	USAF	2.02.01F	C-26 AIRCRAFT FERRY	2	$20,000.00	$16,822.00	$3,178.00	CA17	COMPLETE	Completed Oct 97
	USAF	PC&HCONPUSAF	PC&H CHARGES USAF	1	$32,445.00	$32,445.00	$0.00	CA18	COMPLETE	
	USAF	TRANSCONP USAF	TRANSPORTATION CHARGES USAF	1	$104,288.00	$104,288.00	$0.00	CA19	COMPLETE	
COLOMBIA NV					Sum Of exord value: $9,539,790.00	Sum Of shipments value: $3,874,141.50	Sum Of delta: $5,665,648.50			
	USN	1.11.01	BOSTON WHALER TYPE RIVER BOAT	3	$364,000.00	$111,300.00	$252,700.00	BA21	COMPLETE	Boat cost includes $11,500 per boat for rehab done by USN. Unit cost per boat $25,600.
	USN	1.11.01PCH	PC&H BOSTON WHALER TYPE RIVER BOAT	3	$0.00	$3,000.00	($3,000.00)	BA38	COMPLETE	PC&H for each boat $1,000.00
	USN	1.11.01TRASP	TRANSPORT BOSTON WHALER TYPE RIVER BOAT	3	$0.00	$360,000.00	($360,000.00)	BA39	COMPLETE	Transport cost for each boat $120,000.00
COLOMBIA NV/MC					Sum Of exord value: $364,000.00	Sum Of shipments value: $364,000.00	Sum Of delta: $474,300.00			
	USA	1.09.09	LANDING CRAFT LCU/LCM, 6 MO SPARES & TRAINING	1	$2,000,000.00	$0.00	$2,000,000.00	CC20	CANCEL	ITEM CANCELED BY COUNTRY
	USA	1.09.09PARTS	SHIP PTS COMP&ACRYS	1	$0.00	$2,971.20	($2,971.20)	CC21	COMPLETE	SHIP PARTS/SPARES. 18 REQUISITIONS. 2 KILLED/CANCELED. 16 SHIPPED. SUBTRACTED VALUE FROM EXORD VALUE AUTHORIZED UNDER RCN CC20.
	USA	1.09.10	GPS TRIMBLE	45	$0.00	$0.00	$0.00		CANCEL	CANCELED. NOT AVAILABLE FROM INVENTORY.
	USA	1.09.11	COMPASSES "RITCHIE MARINE"	45	$0.00	$0.00	$0.00		CANCEL	CANCELED. NOT AVAILABLE FROM INVENTORY.
	USA	PC&HCONVMCUSA	PC&H CHARGES USA	1	$1.00	$0.00	$1.00	CC38	COMPLETE	NO REQUISITIONS.
	USA	TRANSCONVMCUSA	TRANSPORTATION CHARGES USA	1	$1.00	$0.00	$1.00	CC39	COMPLETE	NO REQUISITIONS. TRANSPORTATION COSTS RESERVED BY ODMA.
PERU AF					Sum Of exord value: $2,000,002.00	Sum Of shipments value: $2,000,002.00	Sum Of delta: $2,971.20			
	USAF	3.02.01	C-26 A/B AIRCRAFT	4	$12,000,000.00	$3,165,574.00	$8,834,426.00	CA60	COMPLETE	COMPLETE. 2 A/C DEL OCT 97. 2 A/C DEL TO DOS MAY 99.
	USAF	3.02.01F	C-26 A/B AIRCRAFT FERRY	1	$40,000.00	$35,707.00	$4,293.00	CA77	COMPLETE	COMPLETE: OCT 97 & MAY 99.
PERU NP					Sum Of exord value: $12,040,000.00	Sum Of shipments value: $3,201,281.00	Sum Of delta: $8,838,719.00			
	USA	3.03.21	125W TRANSPORTABLE HF RECEIVER 2-30MZ	30	$0.00	$0.00	$0.00		CANCEL	CANCELED. NOT AVAILABLE FROM INVENTORY
	USA	3.03.22	20W SECURE MANPACK PORTABLE RADIOS 2-30MHZ	10	$0.00	$0.00	$0.00		CANCEL	CANCELED. NOT AVAILABLE FROM INVENTORY
	USA	3.03.23	MOUNTS VEHICLE/BOAT FOR 20W 2-30MHZ MANPACK RADIOS	10	$0.00	$0.00	$0.00		CANCEL	CANCELED. NOT AVAILABLE FROM INVENTORY
	USN	1.11.02	BOSTON WHALER TYPE RIVER BOAT	3	$364,000.00	$111,300.00	$252,700.00	BA60	COMPLETE	Boat cost includes $11,500 per boat for rehab done by USN. Unit cost per boat $25,600.
	USN	1.11.02PCH	PC&H BOSTON WHALER TYPE RIVER BOAT	3	$0.00	$3,000.00	($3,000.00)	BA78	COMPLETE	PC&H for each boat $1,000.00
	USN	1.11.02TRANS	TRANSPORT BOSTON WHALER TYPE RIVER BOAT	3	$0.00	$360,000.00	($360,000.00)	BA79	COMPLETE	Transport cost for each boat $120,000.00
VENEZUELA NG					Sum Of exord value: $364,000.00	Sum Of shipments value: $364,000.00	Sum Of delta: $474,300.00			
	USA	5.04.01	LCM-8	1	$2,250,000.00	$174,650.00	$2,075,350.00	CC43	COMPLETE	1 REQUISITION (BVEF0C82459001) SHIPPED. TOTAL COST FOR 1 LCM-8 REPORTED AS $174,650.00.

71

AP5. APPENDIX 5
(PD 99-43 506(a)(2) Counternarcotics Delivery Report)

Customer	Supplier	Line item	Item	Qty	Exord value	Shipments value	Delta	RCN	Delivery status	Shipping notes
	USA	5.04.01PARTS	LCM-8, PTS COMP&ACRYS	1	$3,078.61	$3,078.61	$0.00	CC44	COMPLETE	20 REQUISITIONS: 18 SHIPPED, 2 KILLED/CANCELED.
	USA	PC&HVENGUSA	PC&H CHARGES USA	1	$57,000.00	$57,000.00	$0.00	CC58	COMPLETE	PC&H CHARGES INCURRED PREPARING THE LCM8 FOR SHIPMENT TO VENEZUELA. (RCN duplicate)
	USA	TRANSVENG USA	TRANSPORTATION CHARGES USA	1	$750,000.00	$750,000.00	$0.00	CC59	COMPLETE	TRANSPORTATION CHARGES INCURRED BY THE US ARMY TRANSPORTATION UNIT THAT BARGED THE LCM8 TO VENEZUELA. TRANS COSTS RESER BY ODMA. (RCN duplicate)
	USAF	5.02.01	C-26 A/B AIRCRAFT	2	$6,000,000.00	$2,001,062.00	$3,998,938.00	CC00	COMPLETE	COMPLETE :A/C TRANSFERRED TO DOS JUN 99. LAST A/C DELIVERED 12/99. BOTH AIRCRAFT DELIVERED TO VENEZUELAN AIR FORCE.
	USAF	5.02.01F	C-26 A/B AIRCRAFT FERRY	1	$40,000.00	$21,640.00	$18,360.00	CC01	COMPLETE	COMPLETE: 1ST A/C DELIVERED SEP 99. 2ND DELIVERED 12/99. BOTH AIRCRAFT DELIVERED TO VENEZUELAN AIR FORCE
	USN	5.03.01	MKII PATROL BOATS	6	$295,000.00	$1,155,000.00	($860,000.00)	BA40	COMPLETE	Boat cost includes $12,500 per boat for rehab done by USN. Unit cost per boat $180,000.00.
	USN	5.03.01PCH	PC&H MKII PATROL BOATS	6	$0.00	$6,000.00	($6,000.00)	BA58	COMPLETE	PC&H for each boat $1,000.00
	USN	5.03.01TRANS	TRANSPORT MKII PATROL BOATS	6	$0.00	$120,000.00	($120,000.00)	BA59	COMPLETE	Transport cost for each boat $20,000.00
					Sum Of exord value: $9,395,078.61	Sum Of shipments value: $4,288,430.61	Sum Of delta: $5,106,648.00			
					exord value Grand Total Sum $60,289,477.61	shipments value Grand Total Sum $24,464,404.31				

APPENDIX 6

```
R 032028Z DEC 03
FM SECDEF WASHINGTON DC//USDP-DSCA//
TO USCINCTRANS SCOTT AFB IL//
USCINCUSACOM NORFOLK VA//
USCINCSOC MACDILL AFB FL
DA WASHINGTON DC//SAUS-IA-DSA-SA//
CMC WASHINGTON DC//PLU-SA/FMS//
OSAF WASHINGTON DC//IA/FMB//
HQUSCG WASHINGTON DC//
DLA FT BELVOIR VA//CAIL//FOXS/GC//
DLA FT BELVOIR VA//DLSC-CI/LDM/PPP//
```

SAMPLE EXECUTE ORDER (MODIFIED AND ANNOTATED)

MESSAGE DATE TIME GROUP (DTG) IS ASSIGNED AFTER THE EXORD PACKAGE STAFFING PROCESS IS COMPLETE, THEN THE MESSAGE IS RELEASED.

```
USCINCSO MIAMI FL//SCJ3/SCJ4/SCJ5/SCJ8//
USMILGP BOGOTA CO/LOG//
AMEMBASSY LIMA//
CHMAAG LIMA PE//
AMEMBASSY QUITO//
USMILGP QUITO EC//
AMEMBASSY PANAMA CITY PM//
USMILGP PANAMA CITY PM//
AFSAC WRIGHT PATTERSON AFB OH//IP/CMP/CMA/OMFR//
AFSAC WRIGHT PATTERSON AFB OH//OM/OMFR//
NAVY IPO WASHINGTON DC//280//
CDRUSASAC ALEXANDRIA VA//AMSAC-MA-LA//
DA WASHINGTON DC//DUSA-IA//
JOINT STAFF WASHINGTON DC//DUSA-IA//
INFO SECSTATE WASHINGTON DC//PM-RSAT/INL/ARA//
SECDEF WASHINGTON DC//CHAIRS//
CNO WASHINGTON DC//
CMC WASHINGTON DC//
JOINT STAFF WASHINGTON DC//J5-WHEM/J4-SILD/J3-CNOD /J4-SILD//
USCINCUSACOM//J3/J4/J5/J02L/J02M//
USCINCUSSOUTHCOM//J5/J3-DDD/POLAD//
USCINCSOC MACDILL AFB FL//SOJ5/J4//
USCINCTRANS SCOTT AFB IL//TCJ3/4-ODJ/TCJ8//
DA WASHINGTON DC//DUSA-IA-DSZ/DUSA-IA-DSX//
NAVICP PHILADELPHIA PA//755C//
NAVILCO PHILADELPHIA PA//232/233//
CMC WASHINGTON DC//POS/LPP/LPO//
COMMARCORCYSCOM QUANTICO VA//PSS//
COMNAVSPECWARCOM CORONADO CA//
HQ USAF WASHINGTON DC/ILTT/ILSY/ILSR/ILTV//
HQ AMC SCOTT AFB IL//DON/FMI//DOY//
HQ AMC TACC SCOTT AFB IL//SAMM/DOOM//
CDR TRADOC FT MONROE VA//AFTA-R//
CDRSDDC FALLS CHURCH VA //MTOP-OS//
COMSPECBOATRON TWO//00//
CDRUSASAC NEW CUMBERLAND PA//AMSAC-MA-CM-LA//
AFSAT RANDOLPH AFB TX//CC/TO//
AFMC LSO WRIGHT PATTERSON AFB OH//LOT/LOTA/LOTB//
HQ AFMC WRIGHT PATTERSON AFB OH//LGT/FMRD/FMA/FMACTION OFFICER//
US CUSTOMS SERVICE WASHINGTON
NAVICP MECHANICSBURG PA//OSM//
SECDEF WASHINGTON DC//CHAIRS//
```

CPD MUST TAILOR AUTODIN MESSAGE ADDRESSES FOR DISTRIBUTION ACCORDINGLY. SINCE THE AUTODIN SYSTEM HAS BEEN REPLACED BY THE DEFENSE MESSAGING SYSTEM (DMS), AUTODIN ADDRESS BOOKS ARE NO LONGER DISTRIBUTED. UNTIL DMS BECOMES OPERATIONAL, THE ONLY SOURCE FOR AUTODIN ADDRESS UPDATES (ACP-117) IS THE PENTAGON MESSAGE CENTER AT 703-695-0205/-6055.

```
THIS IS A FOUR PART MESSAGE (PART 1)
SUBJECT: FY99 506(A)(2) DRAWDOWN IN SUPPORT OF ANTI-NARCOTICS
OPERATIONS IN COLOMBIA, PERU, ECUADOR, AND PANAMA. EXECUTE ORDER I.
GENERAL INSTRUCTIONS
REFS:
A. PRESIDENTIAL DETERMINATION (PD)03-15 SIGNED 30 SEPTEMBER 2003
B. DEFENSE TRANSPORTATION REGULATION AND PART TWO-CARGO MOVEMENT, DOD 4500.9-R
C. DOD COMPTROLLER MEMORANDUM DATED 28 JULY 1994, SUBJ: REIMBURSEMENT OF DBOF ACTIVITIES FOR CONTINGENCY
OPERATIONS AND HUMANITARIAN EFFORTS.
D. SOUTHCOM MESSAGE 161910Z DEC 03 TEMPORARY UPGRADE OF FAD FOR COLOMBIA.
```

PART ONE FOR ALL

1. ON 30 SEPTEMBER 2003, THE PRESIDENT SIGNED A PRESIDENTIAL DETERMINATION, REF
OF UP TO $72.55 MILLION OF INVENTORIES AND RESOURCES FROM THE STOCKS OF VARIOUS U
AND MILITARY TRAINING/EDUCATION FROM DOD (AND SPECIFICALLY $69.7 MILLION IN INVENTORIES AND RESOURCES FROM
THE DEPARTMENT OF DEFENSE) UNDER THE AUTHORITY OF SECTION 506(A)(2) OF THE FOREIGN ASSISTANCE ACT (FAA) OF
1961, AS AMENDED, TO SUPPORT COUNTERNARCOTICS ACTIVITIES BY THE GOVERNMENTS OF COLOMBIA, PERU, ECUADOR, AND
PANAMA. THIS MESSAGE DIRECTS ADDRESSEES TO EXECUTE THIS DRAWDOWN AND PROVIDES GENERAL PLANNING
INSTRUCTIONS. IF REQUIRED ADDITIONAL INFORMATION WILL BE PROVIDED IN SUBSEQUENT EXORDS.

2. COUNTRIES SUPPORTED BY THIS EXECUTE ORDER HAVE VALID END USE AGREEMENTS IN ACCORDANCE WITH **SECTION 505**
OF THE FAA (HEREIN AFTER REFERRED TO AS A **'505 AGREEMENT'**THAT ALLOWS FOR THE PROVISION BY DOD OF ANY
INVENTORIES OR RESOURCES UNDER THIS DRAWDOWN. THESE AGREEMENTS SPECIFICALLY ADDRESS END USE OF INVENTORIES
AND RESOURCES PROVIDED UNDER THIS DRAWDOWN AS BEING USED SOLELY FOR COUNTERNARCOTICS PURPOSES. U.S.
COUNTRY TEAMS HAVE BEEN REQUESTED BY THE DEPT. OF STATE TO REVIEW THE DRAWDOWN CONTENT FROM THE POINT OF
VIEW THAT HOST GOVERNMENT PLACEMENT OF THESE ITEMS WILL MEET USG REQUIREMENTS AND THAT EQUIPMENT AND
SERVICES BE USED FOR COUNTER NARCOTICS PURPOSES. COUNTRIES ELIGIBLE TO RECEIVE INVENTORIES AND RESOURCES
FROM THIS DRAWDOWN (I.E. HAVE SIGNED NEW OR AMENDED 505 AGREEMENTS COVERING THE FY99 506 COUNTERNARCOTIC
DRAWDOWN) ARE COLOMBIA, PERU, ECUADOR AND PANAMA. GUIDANCE TO THE SERVICES FOR THE RELEASE OF DOD
INVENTORIES AND RESOURCES TO THESE FOUR COUNTRIES ARE PROVIDED IN THIS EXECUTE ORDER.

3. **ALL INVENTORIES AND RESOURCES PROVIDED UNDER THIS AUTHORITY MUST BE FROM EXISTING STOCKS/RESOURCES.**
NEW PROCUREMENT IS NOT AUTHORIZED UNDER THE PROVISIONS OF SECTION 506(A)(2) OF THE FAA (EXCEPT
TRANSPORTATION AND RELATED SERVICES ACQUIRED BY CONTRACT FOR PURPOSES OF THIS DRAWDOWN IF THE COST IS
LESS EXPENSIVE THAN THE COST TO THE USG OF PROVIDING SERVICES FROM EXISTING AGENCY ASSETS).

4. THE PRESIDENT, THROUGH DOD, IS REQUIRED TO REPORT TO CONGRESS ALL COSTS INCURRED AND DELIVERIES
(PACKING, CRATING, HANDLING, AND TRANSPORTATION) OF COMMODITIES AND SERVICES PROVIDED UNDER THE AUTHORITY
OF THIS PD. THE DSCA 1000 SYSTEM IS THE VEHICLE FOR THIS REPORTING. EACH IMPLEMENTING AGENCY WILL SUBMIT
THE APPROPRIATE PROGRAMMING AND DELIVERY DATA TO THE 1000 SYSTEM AS SOON AS POSSIBLE. GUIDANCE IS PROVIDED
IN CHAPTER 11, SECTION 1102 OF THE SECURITY ASSISTANCE MANAGEMENT MANUAL, DOD 5105.38M. CA
SHOULD CONTAIN THE PRESIDENTIAL DIRECTIVE NUMBER 99-43, AND CARD COLUMN 35 SHOULD CONTAIN

ENTERED INTO THE DSCA 1000 SYSTEM SHOULD BE REVIEWED AND UPDATED AS NECESSARY TO REFLECT TH
OF ANTICIPATED FINAL COSTS. WE CANNOT OVER EMPHASIZE THE IMPORTANCE OF THE NEED FOR IMPLEMEN
TO PROVIDE UPDATES DURING THE COURSE OF THE DRAWDOWN.5. RECORD CONTROL NUMBERS (RCN) WILL
DISCRETELY IDENTIFY THE PROVIDING US MILITARY DEPARTMENT (MILDEP). THE RCN WILL BE USED IN
SUBMISSIONS TO THE DSCA 1000 SYSTEM. DSCA MAY AUTHORIZE REDUCTIONS FROM A SPECIFIC RCN SO THAT DRAWDOWN
AUTHORITY MAY BE RECOUPED AND USED FOR ADDITIONAL REQUIREMENTS. SEPARATE RCNS WILL BE ASSIGNED FOR EACH
LINE VALUE. PROGRAMMING DATA SHOULD BE SUBMITTED BY SERVICES INTO THE DSCA 1000 SYSTEM ASAP.

6. SERVICES WILL ENSURE ALL REQUISITIONS FOR MATERIEL SUBMITTED TO THE SOURCE OF SUPPLY (SOS)/INVENTORY
CONTROL POINT (ICP) CONTAIN:

A. THE SPECIFIC NSN AND QUANTITY NEEDED. STANDARD DOD PRICES REFLECTED IN THE CATALOGING FILE WILL BE USED
TO ACCUMULATE COST DATA ON COMMODITIES/SERVICES FURNISHED UNDER THE RCN.

B. EXCEPT WHERE INDICATED IN THIS OR FUTURE MESSAGES, FORCE ACTIVITY DESIGNATOR THREE **(FAD III)** IS
AUTHORIZED FOR THIS DRAWDOWN AUTHORITY. FORCE ACTIVITY DESIGNATOR TWO (FAD II) IS AUTHORIZED FOR COLOMBIA AS
EQUIPMENT PROVIDED WILL SUPPORT COUNTERNARCOTICS OPERATIONS PER REFERENCE D. ALL REQUISITIONS TO COLOMBIA
SHOULD BE PROCESSED AS FADII. ISSUE PRIORITY DESIGNATOR (IPD) WILL BE IN ACCORDANCE WITH THE AUT
FADS.

C. **FILL OR KILL** ADVICE CODE 2J, 31 OR 33 (AS APPROPRIATE) WILL BE USED (NEW PROCUREMENT IS NOT A
UNDER THE PROVISIONS OF SECTION 506(A)(2)). THIS WILL ENSURE THE ICP PROCESSING REQUISITION WILL
INITIATE NEW PROCUREMENT.

PART TWO - SUPPLY GUIDANCE

7. THE PURPOSE OF THIS SECTION IS TO PROVIDE POLICY AND SUPPLY GUIDANCE AS FOLLOWS:

A. ALL ARTICLES PROVIDED IN THIS DRAWDOWN WILL BE IN AT LEAST CONDITION CODE
B OR -10/-20 STANDARDS, AND FULLY MISSION CAPABLE (NOT DEMILITARIZED'), and UNLESS OTHERWISE INDICATED
DSCA EXECUTE ORDER. ALL ICPS PROCESSING REQUISITIONS WILL ISSUE ON HAND STOCKS IAW CURRENT SUPPLY POLIC
GUIDANCE CONTAINED IN REFERENCE B. END ITEMS WILL BE PROVIDED WITH ALL PUBLICATIONS AND ON BOARD VEHIC
EQUIPMENT/TOOLS ('OEM GEAR') AS WOULD NORMALLY BE ISSUED TO U.S. FORCES.

B. SERVICES ARE AUTHORIZED TO ISSUE BELOW THE REORDER POINT AND MAY IN THE CASE OF MAJOR END ITEMS,
SUBSTITUTE LIKE ITEMS IN ORDER TO FILL REQUIREMENTS. SUBSTITUTIONS OF MAJOR END ITEMS MUST BE PRE-
COORDINATED WITH DSCA POC PRIOR TO SUBSTITUTION.

C. IMPLEMENTING AGENCIES WILL PROCESS ALL REQUISITIONS FOR ANY DEFENSE LOGISTICS AGENCY CONTROLLED
EQUIPMENT. ANY REQUESTS FOR DLA MANAGED SUPPLIES AND SERVICES ARE TO BE FUNDED BY THE REQUESTING
IMPLEMENTING AGENCY. SERVICES SHALL PROVIDE FUND CODES AND 'BILL TO' DODAAC TO DLA PRIOR TO SUBMITTING
REQUISITIONS. THIS INFORMATION SHOULD BE FORWARDED TO DLA-FOXS, TEL: (703) 767-7209, DSN 427-7209 OR
SPARES SHOULD BE REQUISITIONED ON A 'FILL OR KILL' BASIS. FOLLOW-ON GUIDANCE WILL BE PROVIDED FOR SUBSE
PROCESSING OF 'KILLED' CSP REQUISITIONS. DLA IS AUTHORIZED TO FILL REQUISITIONS FOR SECONDARY ITEMS IN
UNIFORM MATERIEL MOVEMENT AND ISSUE PRIORITY SYSTEM (UMMIPS) ISSUE PRIORITY DESIGNATOR (IPD) SEQUENCE AS IF
THE REQUISITIONS ORIGINATED WITH US FORCES. DLA IS AUTHORIZED TO FILL REQUISITIONS BELOW THE REORDER POINT.

D. PROJECT CODE (3JD) HAS BEEN ASSIGNED FOR USE BY ALL SERVICES FOR COMMODITIES AND SERVICES PROVIDED IN ACCORDANCE WITH THIS DRAWDOWN. THIS CODE WILL BE UTILIZED ON ALL SUPPLY AND TRANSPORTATION DOCUMENTATION CONCERNED WITH THIS DRAWDOWN. ALL SHIPPING ACTIVITIES WILL ENSURE THAT THIS PROJECT CODE IS REFLECTED [IN] THE PROJECT CODE FIELD (BLOCK 8) AND THE APPLICABLE MAPAC AND CLEAR TEXT MARK-FOR ADDRESS IS PRINTED IN THE 'MARK FOR' SECTION (BLOCK 9) OF THE MILITARY SHIPMENT LABEL (DD FORM 1387) WHICH IS AFFIXED TO THE OUTSIDE OF EACH SHIPMENT UNIT. SHIPPING ACTIVITIES WILL ENSURE COPIES OF ALL DD FORMS 1348 ARE ENCLOSE[D] IN A PROTECTIVE ENVELOPE AND SECURELY ATTACHED TO THE OUTSIDE OF EACH PACKAGE/CONTAINER. THE RCN SERIE[S] ASSIGNED FOR THIS DRAWDOWN ARE AS INDICATED BELOW. THESE RCNS ARE FOR REPORTING END ITEMS, PC&H, TRANSPORTATION, AND SERVICES.

> CPD MUST OBTAIN A PROJECT CODE FROM J4-SILD SEE C8 4

E. DEPARTMENT OF THE ARMY	RCN SERIES
SUPPORT TO THE COLOMBIAN NATIONAL POLICE	
COMMODITIES/SERVICES	AA00–AA17
PC&H	AA18
TRANSPORTATION	AA19
SUPPORT TO THE COLOMBIAN MILITARY	
COMMODITIES AND SERVICES	AA20–AA37
PC&H	AA38
TRANSPORTATION	AA39
SUPPORT TO THE PERUVIAN MILITARY	
COMMODITIES AND SERVICES	AA40–AA57
PC&H	AA58
TRANSPORTATION	AA59
SUPPORT TO THE PERUVIAN POLICE	
COMMODITIES AND SERVICES	AA60–AA77
PC&H	AA78
TRANSPORTATION	AA79
SUPPORT TO THE ECUADORIAN MILITARY	
COMMODITIES AND SERVICES	AA80–AA97
PC&H	AA98
TRANSPORTATION	AA99
SUPPORT TO THE ECUADORIAN POLICE	
COMMODITIES AND SERVICES	AB01–AB17
PC&H	AB18
TRANSPORTATION	AB19
SUPPORT TO THE PANAMANIAN POLICE	
COMMODITIES AND SERVICES	AB40–57
PC&H	AB58
TRANSPORTATION	AB59

> CPD MUST OBTAIN FROM DSCA COMPTROLLER'S OFFICE THE RCN BLOCK'S FOR EACH MILDEP PROVIDING COMMODITIES/SERVICES ASSIGNED RCN BLOCKS SHOULD BE LARGE ENOUGH TO ACCOMMODATE ALL LINE ITEMS ASSIGNED TO EACH COUNTRY/SERVICE(S), AND SHOULD INCLUDE NUMBERS FOR PC&H AND TRANSPORTATION SEE C9 5 AND C8 11

F. DEPARTMENT OF THE NAVY: RCN SERIES:	
SUPPORT TO THE COLOMBIAN NATIONAL POLICE	
COMMODITIES/SERVICES	AB60–AB77
PC&H	AB78
TRANSPORTATION	AB79
SUPPORT TO THE COLOMBIAN MILITARY	
COMMODITIES/SERVICES	AB80–AB97
PC&H	AB98
TRANSPORTATION	AB99
SUPPORT TO THE PERUVIAN MILITARY	
COMMODITIES AND SERVICES	AC01–AC17
PC&H	AC18
TRANSPORTATION	AC19
SUPPORT TO THE PERUVIAN POLICE	
COMMODITIES/SERVICES	AC20–AC37
PC&H	AC38
TRANSPORTATION	AC39
SUPPORT TO THE ECUADORIAN MILITARY	
COMMODITIES/SERVICES	AC40–AC57
PC&H	AC58
TRANSPORTATION	AC59
SUPPORT TO THE ECUADORIAN POLICE	
COMMODITIES/SERVICES	AC60–AC77
PC&H	AC78
TRANSPORTATION	AC79
SUPPORT TO THE PANAMANIAN NATIONAL MARITIME POLICE SERVICE	
COMMODITIES/SERVICES	AD01–AD17
PC&H	AD18
TRANSPORTATION	AD19

G. DEPARTMENT OF THE AIR FORCE	
SUPPORT TO THE COLOMBIAN NATIONAL POLICE	
COMMODITIES/SERVICES	AD20–AD37

```
                    PC&H                                AD38
                    TRANSPORTATION                      AD39
          SUPPORT TO THE COLOMBIAN MILITARY
                    COMMODITIES/SERVICES                AD40-AD57
                    PC&H                                AD58
                    TRANSPORTATION                      AD59
          SUPPORT TO THE PERUVIAN MILITARY
                    COMMODITIES/SERVICES                AD60-AD77
                    PC&H                                AD78
                    TRANSPORTATION                      AD79
          SUPPORT TO THE PERUVIAN POLICE
                    COMMODITIES/SERVICES                AD80-AD97
                    PC&H                                AD98
                    TRANSPORTATION                      AD99
          SUPPORT TO THE ECUADORIAN MILITARY
                    COMMODITIES/SERVICES                AE01-AE17
                    PC&H                                AE18
                    TRANSPORTATION                      AE19
          SUPPORT TO THE ECUADORIAN POLICE
                    COMMODITIES/SERVICES                AE20-AE37
                    PC&H                                AE38
                    TRANSPORTATION                      AE39
          SUPPORT TO THE PANAMANIAN POLICE
                    COMMODITIES/SERVICES                AE60-AE77
                    PC&H                                AE78
                    TRANSPORTATION                      AE79
```

> PD DRAWDOWN AUTHORITY MUST NOT BE EXCEEDED SEE C11 1

H. **TOTAL DRAWDOWN AUTHORITY AUTHORIZED BY THE PRESIDENTIAL DETERMINATION FOR DOD IS $69.7 MILLION. NO LEGAL AUTHORITY EXISTS TO PROVIDE IN EXCESS OF $69.7 MILLION OF DOD INVENTORIES AND RESOURCES UNDER THE AUTHORITY OF THIS DRAWDOWN. UNDER NO CIRCUMSTANCES WILL THIS ALLOCATION BE EXCEEDED.**

I. SERVICES WILL ADVISE SECDEF/USDP: DSCA (ERASA/ASA/COMP) IF ANY GOODS AND/OR SERVICES REQUESTED ARE UNAVAILABLE FOR DRAWDOWN BY FRONT CHANNEL MESSAGE INFO APPROPRIATE ACTION ADDRESSEES ON THIS MESSAGE, WITHIN SEVEN DAYS OF RECEIPT OF THIS OR SUCCEEDING DSCA EXORDS. THE CRITERIA FOR NON-AVAILABILITY IS THAT THE ITEM IS NOT IN STOCK OR THE DRAWDOWN OF THE SPECIFIC GOODS/SERVICES FROM MILDEP STOCKS WILL HAVE A SEVERE DETRIMENTAL IMPACT ON THE OPERATIONAL READINESS OF THEIR MILITARY DEPARTMENT. EXTENSIVE PRE-COORDINATION WITH SERVICES, ICPS, STATE DEPT. AND CONGRESS SHOULD PRECLUDE NON-AVAILABILITY OF ITEMS CALLED FOR IN THIS OR SUBSEQUENT EXORDS. DRAWDOWN OF THE GOODS/SERVICES MAY NEVERTHELESS BE REQUIRED OR MODIFIED BY SUBSEQUENT EXECUTE ORDER.

J. AS PREVIOUSLY COORDINATED WITH THE SERVICES, COUNTRIES AUTHORIZED TO RECEIVE TRAINING UNDER THIS DRAWDOWN, WILL, IF THIS TRAINING IS DETERMINED TO BE UNAVAILABLE AT THE TIME OF THE TRAINING REQUEST, RECEIVE INSTEAD, OTHER GOODS OR SERVICES AS DIRECTED BY THE APPLICABLE EXECUTE ORDER. TRAINING REQUESTS AUTHORIZED UNDER THIS DRAWDOWN WILL BE MADE BY THE COUNTRY TEAM UTILIZING GUIDANCE AND FORMATS OUTLINED THE JOINT SECURITY ASSISTANCE TRAINING (JSAT) REGULATION, AR 12-15/SECNAVINST 4950.4/AFR50-29.

PART THREE - TRANSPORTATION GUIDANCE

8. THE PURPOSE OF THIS SECTION IS TO PROVIDE TRANSPORTATION GUIDANCE:

A. IAW REF C., TRANSPORTATION WILL BE ABSORBED BY THE MILDEP PROVIDING THE COMMODITY/SERVICE OR TRAINING AS PART OF THE DRAWDOWN. UNDER THE PROVISIONS OF SECTION 506(A)(2) FOREIGN ASSISTANCE ACT, SERVICES MAY MAKE FULL USE OF COMMERCIAL CONTRACT TRANSPORTATION SERVICES INCLUDING THE USE OF NEW CONTRACTS IF THE COST IS LESS THAN USING READILY-AVAILABLE DEFENSE TRANSPORTATION SYSTEM ASSETS (CONSIDERING URGENCY OF SHIPMENT). COSTS OF CARGO PREPARATION, PACKAGING, AND SHIPPING TO ULTIMATE DESTINATION WILL ALSO BE ABSORBED BY SERVICES AS PART OF THIS DRAWDOWN AND REPORTED USING APPROPRIATE RCNS SHOWN ABOVE.

. STANDARD DOD PROCEDURES WILL BE USED TO SUBMIT TRANSPORTATION REQUIREMENTS. SERVICES WILL ADDRESS, ELEASE AND SHIP MATERIEL IN ACCORDANCE WITH CURRENT MILSTRIP, MILSTAMP AND MAPAD PROCEDURES. SERVICES WI UND TRANSPORTATION IAW REFERENCE C.

. TO MINIMIZE COSTS AND FACILITATE RECEIPT AND DISTRIBUTION IN HOST NATIONS, A SINGLE **CONSOLIDATION POIN** T NAVICE/OSM, MECHANICSBURG, PA WILL BE SET UP FOR NON-SENSITIVE ITEMS AND USED TO THE MAXIMUM EXTENT POSSIBLE. IN-COUNTRY U.S. MILITARY REPRESENTATIV ILL COORDINATE WITH U.S. SPONSORING SERVICE SECURITY ASSISTANCE AGENCY PERSONNEL TO ESTABLISH MAPAD DDRESSES THAT WILL AFFECT USE OF THE CONSOLIDATION POINT. WHEN POSSIBLE, REQUISITIONS/MROS WILL BE UBMITTED WITH THE APPROPRIATE ADDRESS DATA IN THEM THAT WILL GENERATE SHIPMENTS TO THE CONSOLIDATION POINT ND STATUS REPORTS TO THE IN-COUNTRY U.S. MILITARY REPRESENTATIVES. THE CONSOLIDATION POINT WILL RELEASE ATERIEL IN ACCORDANCE WITH CALL-FORWARD INSTRUCTIONS FROM THE U.S. MILITARY REPRESENTATIVES AND U.S. PONSORING SERVICE SECURITY ASSISTANCE AGENCIES. THE CALL-FORWARD INSTRUCTIONS WILL DETERMINE WHETHER URFACE OR AIR TRANSPORTATION SHOULD BE USED. SHIPMENTS OF SENSITIVE ITEMS (I.E. EAPONS/AMMUNITION/PYROTECHNICS/EXPLOSIVES) WILL BE HANDLED IAW WITH STANDARD PROCEDURES FOR THOSE TYPES OF TEMS.

. STANDARD DOD MARKING AND LABELING PROCEDURES PRESCRIBED BY MIL-STD-129 AND DOD 4500.32R (MILSTAMP) WILL E USED.

. DOD TRANSPORTATION RATES WILL BE USED FOR DRAWDOWN ACCOUNTING.

. U.S. MILITARY REPRESENTATIVES IN EACH RECIPIENT COUNTRY WILL ESTABLISH MAPAD ADDRESSES THAT WILL ENSURE ECEIPT BY THEM OF SUPPLY AND TRANSPORTATION STATUS AND DOCUMENTATION AS UPDATES OCCUR. BASED ON STATUS, HE U.S. MILITARY REPRESENTATIVE WILL COORDINATE WITH THE RESPECTIVE U.S. SPONSORING SERVICE SECURITY SSISTANCE AGENCIES FOR EXPEDITING OR CALL-FORWARD OF CONSOLIDATION POINT MATERIEL AS REQUIRED.

> CPD SHOULD DETERMINE THE COST/BENEFIT OF USING A CONSOLIDATION POINT IF ONE IS DESIGNATED, THE CPD SHALL COORDINATE UP FRONT WITH SERVICES AND RECEIVING COUNTRY (IES) ISSUES SUCH AS SHIPMENT SCHEDULES, MAPAC UPDATES, CONSOLIDATION POINT PAYMENT SCHEDULES ETC SEE C9 9

G. STATUS AND SUPPLY/TRANSPORTATION DOCUMENTATION WILL FLOW TO THE IN-COUNTRY U.S. MILREPS IN ACCORDANCE WITH MILSTRIP AND MILSTAMP PROCEDURES TO ADDRESSES ESTABLISHED IN THE MAPAD. ANY DIFFICULTIES WITH RECEIPT OF STATUS AND DOCUMENTATION SHOULD BE RESOLVED WITH THE RESPECTIVE U.S. SPONSORING SERVICE SECURITY ASSISTANCE AGENCIES AND THE INVOLVED TRANSPORTATION AGENCY (IE SDDC). THE SDDC POC FOR MILGROUPS TO COORDINATE EXPRESS AIR SHIPMENT OF ORIGINAL SHIPPING DOCUMENTS IS MR. STEVE KOVAL AT FT. EUSTIS DEPLOYMENT SUPPORT COMMAND, COMM 757-878-8627.

H. ALL SHIPMENTS WILL BE UNCLASSIFIED UNLESS OTHERWISE INDICATED.

I. INTERNATIONAL SMALL PARCEL EXPEDITED SERVICES (E.G. FEDEX) WILL NOT BE USED UNLESS REQUESTED BY AN IN-COUNTRY U.S. MILITARY REPRESENTATIVE TO EXPEDITE A SPECIAL URGENT REQUIREMENT.

J. FOR COORDINATION PURPOSES ONLY, FOLLOWING ARE TRANSPORTATION/DELIVERY POINTS OF CONTACT (POCS): FOR AMEMBASSY COLOMBIA CAPT BARRY BREWER OR MS. MARCELA FORERO, COMM 571-244-2784 OR 2785,CELL 573-261-2144 (BREWER) OR 573-226-6069 (FORERO), EMAIL BREWERB@BOGOTA.MG.SOUTHCOM.MIL OR FOREROM@BOGOTA.MG.SOUTHCOM.MIL. FOR AMEMBASSY ECUADOR, POCS ARE SFC JOSE J. BOWIE OR MS. VERONICA EGUEZ (MAIN POC), COMM 593-250-4151 0R 4152 EMAIL BOWIEJ@QUITO.MG.SOUTHCOM.MIL OR EGUEZV@QUITO.MG.SOUTHCOM.MIL. FOR AMEMBASSY PERU, POCS ARE MAJ STEPHEN WHITT OR MS CECILIA DE VIGO, COMM 511-434-3000, EXT 2294/2289, EMAIL WHITTA@LIMA.MG.SOUTHCOM.MIL OR VIGOC@LIMA.MG.SOUTHCOM.MIL. POCS FOR AMEMBASSY PANAMA ARE CDR STEVE MOREHEAD, COMM 507-227-1777 OR DSN 313-285-4605, EMAIL SMOREHEAD@SAN.OSD.MIL, OR MAJ BILL DOONER COMM 507-207-7408, EMAIL DOONERWJ@STATE.GOV. FOR SOUTHCOM MR SCOTT MURRAY, COMM 305-437-3662,EMAIL USCJ4SILD@HQ.SOUTHCOM.MIL. FOR NAVICP/OSM MR.DAVID CECIL, COMM717-605-1442, EMAIL DAVID_J_CECIL@ICPMECH.NAVY.MIL, MR. LARRY JACOBS, 717-605-3528 COMM 717-605-3528, EMAIL LAWRENCE_S_JACOBS@ICPMECH.NAVY.MIL.

PART FOUR FOR DEPARTMENTS OF THE ARMY, NAVY AND AIR FORCE

9. THE FOLLOWING SECTION IS PROVIDED FOR MILDEP PLANNERS TO BEGIN EXECUTION OF THIS DRAWDOWN. QUANTITIES, WHERE SHOWN, WERE ESTIMATED BY MILDEP PLANNERS. WHERE NO QUANTITY IS SHOWN, SERVICES ARE REQUESTED TO SHIP QUANTITIES AVAILABLE UP TO THE FUNDING THRESHOLD PROVIDED FOR IN THAT CATEGORY. **FOR WEAPONS, AMMUNITION, EXPLOSIVES AND PYROTECHNICS SERVICES MUST COORDINATE WITH MILGROUPS TO DETERMINE SPECIFIC DODAC REQUIREMENTS AND WEAPON TYPE/MODELS TO AVOID COMPATIBILITY/OPERATIONAL PROBLEMS.** UNDER NO CIRCUMSTANCES WILL THE DOLLAR VALUE SHOWN IN ANY CATEGORY BE EXCEEDED UNLESS APPROVED BY DSCA AND DOCUMENTED IN A SUBSEQUENT EXECUTE ORDER. THE COUNTRIES ELIGIBLE TO RECEIVE INVENTORIES AND RESOURCES FROM THIS DRAWDOWN (I.E. HAVE SIGNED A NEW OR AMENDED 505 AGREEMENTS COVERING THE FY99 506 COUNTERNARCOTICS DRAWDOWN) ARE COLOMBIA, PERU, ECUADOR AND PANAMA.

9A. DEPARTMENT OF THE ARMY IS AUTHORIZED TO PROVIDE THE COLOMBIAN NATIONAL POLICE, UNDER SEC 506(A)(2) AUTHORITY, THE FOLLOWING STOCKS, SERVICES AND/OR TRAINING. REQUEST DELIVERY OF THE FOLLOWING INVENTORY AND RESOURCES TO THE COLOMBIAN NATIONAL POLICE:

ITEM	QUANTITY	VALUE
- UH 60 SPARE PARTS	VARIOUS	$ 2,000,000
- M-79	100	$ 79,000
- M60 MG	50	$ 700,000
- SPARE PARTS FOR M60 MG		$ 200,000
- THERMITE GRENADES	1000	$ 20,000
- 7.62 LINKED FOR M60 MG		$ 2,250,000

(ARMY WILL COORDINATE AMMUNITION DODAC REQUIREMENTS/AVAILABILITY WITH RECEIVING NATION MILGROUP POC PRIOR TO PROCESSING REQUISITIONS/SHIPMENTS)

- MOBILE TRAINING TEAMS 4		
-- HOW TO MAINTAIN AIRCRAFT LIFE SUPPORT SYSTEMS		$ 15,000
-- INSTRUCTIONS ON WEAPONS HANDLING MAINTENANCE AND STORAGE		$ 18,000
-- AIR DEFENSE AND FORCE PROTECTION		$ 80,000
-- EVALUATION AND INSTRUCTION ON TACTICAL COMMUNICATION		$ 180,000

TOTAL DRAWDOWN AUTHORITY PROVIDED BY THE DEPARTMENT OF THE ARMY FOR THE COLOMBIAN NATIONAL POLICE BY THIS EXECUTE ORDER NOT TO EXCEED $5,542,000

DEPARTMENT OF THE ARMY IS AUTHORIZED TO PROVIDE THE COLOMBIAN MILITARY, UNDER SECTION 506(A)(AUTHORITY, THE FOLLOWING STOCKS, SERVICES AND/OR TRAINING. REQUEST DELIVERY OF THE FOLLOWING INVENTORY AND RESOURCES TO THE COLOMBIAN MILITARY:

ITEM	QUANTITY	VALUE
- UH 60 SPARE PARTS (COLAR 1/3,FAC 2/3)	VARIOUS	$ 6,000,000
- 81MM MORTARS WITH EQUIP (COLAR 80%, COLMAR 20%)	20	$ 460,000
- M-79 (COLAR 50%, COLMAR 50%)	300	$ 247,000
- M60 MACHINE-GUNS (COLAR 40%, COLMAR 40%, FAC 20%)	150	$ 700,000
- 7.62 LINKED FOR M60 MG (COLAR, COLMAR, FAC ALLOCATION TBD)		$ 1,050,000

Margin notes:

WHEN APPLICABLE, MILGROUPS SUBMIT UPDATED MAPAC'S (TAC-M) TO ASSURE THE DELIVERY OF ORIGINAL SHIPPING DOCUMENTS NEEDED TO CLEAR MATERIEL THROUGH CUSTOMS.

CPD MUST MAKE SURE MILDEP AND MILGROUP COORDINATE THE REQUIREMENTS TO AVOID COMPATIBILITY PROBLEMS/ISSUES

LIST EACH MILDEP REQUIREMENT IN A SEPARATE ENTRY

DRAWDOWNS **DO NOT** PROVIDE OBLIGATIONAL AUTHORITY USE **DRAWDOWN AUTHORITY** THROUGHOUT THE EXORD SEE C1 2 4

(ARMY WILL COORDINATE AMMUNITION DODAC REQUIREMENTS/AVAILABILITY WITH RECEIVING
NATION MILGROUP POC PRIOR TO PROCESSING REQUISITIONS/SHIPMENTS)
- 81MM MORTAR AMMO   10,000 $1,410,000
  (COLAR 80%, COLMAR 20%)
(ARMY WILL COORDINATE AMMUNITION DODAC REQUIREMENTS/AVAILABILITY WITH RECEIVING
NATION MILGROUP POC PRIOR TO PROCESSING REQUISITIONS/SHIPMENTS)
- 40MM AMMO FOR M-79 $2,054,000
  (COLAR 50%, COLMAR 50%)
(ARMY WILL COORDINATE AMMUNITION DODAC REQUIREMENTS/AVAILABILITY WITH RECEIVING
NATION MILGROUP POC PRIOR TO PROCESSING REQUISITIONS/SHIPMENTS)
- THERMITE GRENADES   1000 $ 20,000
  (COLAR 100%)
- MOBILE TRAINING TEAMS
  -- INSTRUCTIONS FOR SEARCH   1 $ 80,000
     AND RESCUE OPERATIONS
  -- INSTRUCTIONS FOR SECURITY 1 $ 80,000
     FORCE TRAINING
- FIELD DEFENSIVE   EQUIPMENT NOT TO EXCEED $2,000,000
(COLAR 40%, COLMAR 40%, FAC 20%)
- FLIGHT EQUIPMENT NOT TO EXCEED $ 650,000
  --(COLAR 65%, COLNAV 35%)
TOTAL DRAWDOWN AUTHORITY PROVIDED BY THE DEPARTMENT OF THE ARMY FOR THE COLOMBIAN MILITARY BY
THIS EXECUTE ORDER NOT TO EXCEED: $14,751,000

DEPARTMENT OF THE ARMY IS AUTHORIZED TO PROVIDE USMILGROUP COLOMBIA, UNDER SECTION 506(A)(2)
AUTHORITY, THE FOLLOWING SERVICE. REQUEST DELIVERY OF THE FOLLOWING SERVICE TO USMILGROUP
COLOMBIA:

ITEM   VALUE
LOGISTICIAN (TDY) TO SUPPORT OPERATIONS AT USMILGROUP
COLOMBIA $60,000

NOTES: TDY NOT TO EXCEED 180 DAYS. USMILGROUP COLOMBIA WILL COORDINATE DETAILS OF TDY DATES AND
CALL-UP MESSAGE REQUIREMENTS WITH THE ARMY.

TOTAL DRAWDOWN AUTHORITY PROVIDED BY THE DEPARTMENT OF THE ARMY FOR USMILGROUP COLOMBIA BY THIS
EXECUTE ORDER
NOT TO EXCEED $60,000

DEPARTMENT OF THE ARMY IS AUTHORIZED TO PROVIDE THE PERUVIAN NATIONAL POLICE, UNDER SECTION
506(A)(2) AUTHORITY, THE FOLLOWING STOCKS, SERVICES AND/OR TRAINING. REQUEST DELIVERY OF THE
FOLLOWING INVENTORY AND RESOURCES TO THE PERUVIAN NATIONAL POLICE:

        ITEM   QUANTITY   VALUE
- AVIATION LIFE SUPPORT
  NOT TO EXCEED: $ 600,000
  -- FLIGHT HELMETS   50
  -- HEADSET MICROPHONES
     (H-15A/ATC)   30
  -- FLYER COVERALLS   200
  -- FLYER GLOVES   200
  -- FLYER BOOTS   100
  -- SAFETY BOOTS   100
  -- LIFE PRESERVERS   100
  -- 50 SURVIVAL RADIOS
     (PRC-90)   50
  -- HELO EMERGENCY EGRESS
     DEVICE SYSTEMS BTLS   200
  -- JACKETS FLYER SUMMER
     WEIGHT   50
  -- JACKETS FLYER WINTER
     WEIGHT   50
  -- HOT CLIMATE SURVIVAL
     KITS   20
  -- MRES CASES   900
  -- 5500LB CAPABLE
     CARABINERS (LOCKING
     SNAP-LINK)   100
- AVIATION REFUEL KITS   5 $ 600,000
TOTAL DRAWDOWN AUTHORITY PROVIDED BY THE DEPARTMENT OF THE ARMY FOR THE PERUVIAN NATIONAL POLICE
BY
THIS EXECUTE ORDER NOT TO EXCEED: $1,200,000

DEPARTMENT OF THE ARMY IS AUTHORIZED TO PROVIDE THE ECUADORIAN MILITARY UNDER SECTION 506(A)(2)
AUTHORITY, THE FOLLOWING STOCKS, SERVICES AND/OR TRAINING. REQUEST DELIVERY OF THE FOLLOWING
INVENTORY AND RESOURCES TO THE ECUADORIAN MILITARY:

```
ITEM                 QUANTITY           VALUE
- 9MM BALL AMMO                         $  500,000
  (2/3 MILITARY, 1/3 POLICE)
```
(ARMY WILL COORDINATE AMMUNITION DODAC REQUIREMENTS/AVAILABILITY WITH RECEIVING NATION MILGROUP
POC PRIOR TO PROCESSING REQUISITIONS/SHIPMENTS)
TOTAL DRAWDOWN AUTHORITY PROVIDED BY THE DEPARTMENT OF THE ARMY FOR THE ECUADORIAN MI[

THIS EXECUTE ORDER NOT TO EXCEED: $ 500,000

TOTAL TRANSPORTATION DRAWDOWN AUTHORITY FOR ARMY PROVIDED FOR
THIS PD IS: $ 1,155,666

TOTAL DRAWDOWN AUTHORITY PROVIDED BY THE DEPARTMENT OF THE ARMY
THIS EXECUTE ORDER NOT TO EXCEED: $ 23,208,666

> DRAWDOWNS **DO NOT** PROVIDE OBLIGATIONAL AUTHORITY USE **DRAWDOWN AUTHORITY** THROUGHOUT THE EXORD SEE C1 2 4

> LIST EACH MILDEP REQUIREMENT IN A SEPARATE ENTRY.

XXXXXXXXXXXXXXXXXXXXXXXXXXXXXXXXXXXXXXXXXXXXXXXXXXXXXXXXXXXXXXXX

9B. DEPARTMENT OF THE NAVY IS AUTHORIZED TO PROVIDE THE COLOMBIAN NATIONAL POLICE, UNDER SECTION
506(A)(2) AUTHORITY, THE FOLLOWING STOCKS, SERVICES AND/OR TRAINING. REQUEST DELIVERY OF THE
FOLLOWING INVENTORY AND RESOURCES TO THE COLOMBIAN NATIONAL POLICE:

```
ITEM                 QUANTITY           VALUE
- LOT:FIELD GEAR
  NOT TO EXCEED           1             $  341,000
  -- LBE, BOOTS
     CANTEENS, RAIN GEAR BACK PACKS, COMPASSES AMMO POUCHES
- LOT:FIELD DEFENSIVE
  EQUIPMENT NOT TO EXCEED 1             $  282,000
- LOT:FUEL                1             $2,000,000
```
(SEE DETAILED INSTRUCTIONS ON PARAGRAPH 10)
TOTAL DRAWDOWN AUTHORITY PROVIDED BY THE DEPARTMENT OF THE NAVY FOR THE COLOMBIAN NATIONAL POLICE
BY
THIS EXECUTE ORDER NOT TO EXCEED: $2,623,000

DEPARTMENT OF THE NAVY IS AUTHORIZED TO PROVIDE THE COLOMBIAN MILITARY, UNDER SECTION 506(A)(2)
AUTHORITY, THE FOLLOWING STOCKS, SERVICES AND/OR TRAINING
REQUEST DELIVERY OF THE FOLLOWING INVENTORY AND RESOURCES TO THE COLOMBIAN MILITARY:

```
ITEM                 QUANTITY           VALUE
- LOT:UH-1N SPARES   VARIOUS            $5,000,000
  (COLAR 100%)
- LOT:FUEL                1             $7,500,000
  (SEE DETAILED INSTRUCTIONS ON PARAGRAPH 10)
- LOT:5.56 M16 AMMO       1             $  630,000
  (COLAR 30%,COLMAR 50%, FAC 20%)
```
(NAVY WILL COORDINATE AMMUNITION DODAC REQUIREMENTS/AVAILABILITY WITH RECEIVING NATION MILGROUP
POC PRIOR TO PROCESSING REQUISITIONS/SHIPMENTS)
```
- MOBILE TRAINING TEAMS
  -- INSTRUCTION FOR
     UH1N MAINTENANCE
     AND LOGISTICS                      $  100,000
- INSTRUCTION IN OPS AND MAINTENANCE OF NVG
  SYSTEMS                 4             $  200,000
- EXTENDED TRAINING SERVICE SPECIALISTS (ETSS) (COLOMBIAN ARMY)USMC MAJOR OPERATIONS DIRECTOR FOR
UH1N
  PROGRAM                 1             $  400,000
- FIELD RATIONS                         $  500,000
  (COLAR 70%, COLMAR 30%)
- FIELD GEAR
  NOT TO EXCEED                         $1,200,000
  (COLAR 40%,COLMAR 35%,FAC 25%)
  -- LBE, BOOTS, RAIN GEAR, CANTEENS BACK PACKS, COMPASSES AMMO POUCHES
```
TOTAL DRAWDOWN AUTHORITY PROVIDED BY THE DEPARTMENT OF THE NAVY FOR THE COLOMBIAN MILITARY BY
THIS EXECUTE ORDER NOT TO EXCEED: $15,530,000

DEPARTMENT OF THE NAVY IS AUTHORIZED TO PROVIDE THE PERUVIAN MILITARY, UNDER SECTION 506(A)(2)
AUTHORITY, THE FOLLOWING STOCKS, SERVICES AND/OR TRAINING REQUEST DELIVERY OF THE FOLLOWING
INVENTORY AND RESOURCES TO THE PERUVIAN MILITARY:

```
ITEM                 QUANTITY           VALUE
```

APPENDIX 6

```
- LOT FUEL                1                $1,000,000
(SEE DETAILED INSTRUCTIONS ON PARAGRAPH 10)
TOTAL DRAWDOWN AUTHORITY PROVIDED BY THE DEPARTMENT OF THE NAVY FOR THE PERUVIAN MILITARY BY
THIS EXECUTE ORDER NOT TO EXCEED:        $1,000,000

DEPARTMENT OF THE NAVY IS AUTHORIZED TO PROVIDE THE ECUADORIAN MILITARY, UNDER SECTION 506(A)(2)
AUTHORITY, THE FOLLOWING STOCKS, SERVICES AND/OR TRAINING.  REQUEST DELIVERY OF THE FOLLOWING
INVENTORY AND RESOURCES TO THE ECUADORIAN MILITARY:

ITEM                QUANTITY              VALUE
- M16A1             1500                  $ 750,000
  (MILITARY 1000 /POLICE 500)
- 5.56 BALL/TRACER AMMO                   $ 300,000
  (2/3 MILITARY 1/3 POLICE)
(NAVY WILL COORDINATE AMMUNITION DODAC REQUIREMENTS/AVAILABILITY WITH RECEIVING NATION MILGROUP
POC PRIOR TO PROCESSING REQUISITIONS/SHIPMENTS)
TOTAL DRAWDOWN AUTHORITY PROVIDED BY THE DEPARTMENT OF THE NAVY FOR THE ECUADORIAN MILITARY BY
THIS EXECUTE ORDER NOT TO EXCEED:        $1,050,000

DEPARTMENT OF THE NAVY IS AUTHORIZED TO PROVIDE THE PANAMANIAN NATIONAL MARITIME POLICE SERVICE,
UNDER SECTION 506(A)(2) AUTHORITY, THE FOLLOWING STOCKS, SERVICES AND/OR TRAINING. REQUEST
DELIVERY OF THE FOLLOWING INVENTORY AND RESOURCES TO THE PANAMANIAN NATIONAL MARITIME POLICE
SERVICE:

ITEM                QUANTITY              VALUE
- UTILITY BOATS     2                     $ 250,000
  41FT
TOTAL DRAWDOWN AUTHORITY PROVIDED BY THE DEPARTMENT OF THE NAVY FOR THE PANAMANIAN NATIONAL
MARITIME POLICE SERVICE BY THIS EXECUTE ORDER
NOT TO EXCEED:                           $ 250,000

TOTAL TRANSPORTATION DRAWDOWN AUTHORITY FOR NAVY PROVIDED FOR
THIS PD IS:                              $ 2,755,667

TOTAL DRAWDOWN AUTHORITY PROVIDED BY THE DEPARTMENT OF THE NAVY
THIS EXECUTE ORDER NOT TO EXCEED:        $23,208,667

XXXXXXXXXXXXXXXXXXXXXXXXXXXXXXXXXXXXXXXXXXXXXXXXXXXXXXXXXXXXXXXXXX
```

LIST EACH MILDEP REQUIREMENT IN A SEPARATE ENTRY

```
9C.  DEPARTMENT OF THE AIR FORCE IS AUTHORIZED TO PROVIDE THE COLOMBIAN NATIONAL POLICE  UNDER
SECTION 506(A)(2) AUTHORITY, THE FOLLOWING STOCKS, SERVICES AND/OR TRAINING.  REQUEST DELIVER
THE FOLLOWING INVENTORY AND RESOURCES TO THE COLOMBIAN NATIONAL POLICE:

ITEM                QUANTITY              VALUE
- M16 BASIC RIFLES  500                   $   62,500
- 50 CAL LINKED     5MIL RDS              $1,650,000
(AIR FORCE WILL COORDINATE AMMUNITION DODAC REQUIREMENTS/AVAILABILITY WITH RECEIVING NATION
MILGROUP POC PRIOR TO PROCESSING REQUISITIONS/SHIPMENTS)
- RUNWAY CRATERING  50                    $   35,000
  CHARGES
- FLIGHT EQUIPMENT
  NOT TO EXCEED                           $  400,000
  -- HELMETS
  -- FLIGHT SUITS
  -- GLOVES
  -- SURVIVAL GEAR
  -- FLAK VESTS
  -- 9MM PISTOL HOLSTERS
  -- FLARE PISTOLS
  -- FLASHLIGHTS
  -- OXYGEN MASK
- LOT: FUEL         1                     $1,000,000
(SEE DETAILED INSTRUCTIONS ON PARAGRAPH 10)
TOTAL DRAWDOWN AUTHORITY PROVIDED BY THE DEPARTMENT OF THE AIR FORCE FOR THE COLOMBIAN NATIONAL
POLICE BY
THIS EXECUTE ORDER NOT TO EXCEED         $3,147,500

DEPARTMENT OF THE AIR FORCE IS AUTHORIZED TO PROVIDE THE COLOMBIAN MILITARY, UNDER SECTION
506(A)(2) AUTHORITY, THE FOLLOWING STOCKS, SERVICES AND/OR TRAINING.  REQUEST DELIVERY OF THE
FOLLOWING INVENTORY AND RESOURCES TO THE COLOMBIAN MILITARY:

ITEM                QUANTITY              VALUE
- UH1N'S SPARE PARTS  VARIOUS             $5,000,000
```

```
    (COLAR 100%)
- A-37 SPARE PARTS      VARIOUS            $2,200,000
   (FAC 100%)
- C-130 SPARE PARTS     VARIOUS            $1,180,000
   (FAC 100%)
- M16 BASIC RIFLES      1500          $    187,500
(COLAR, COLNAV, FAC ALLOCATIONS TBD)
- .50 CAL LINKED        5MIL RDS           $1,650,000
   (COLAR/COLMAR/FAC BREAKDOWN TBD)
(AIR FORCE WILL COORDINATE AMMUNITION DODAC REQUIREMENTS/AVAILABILITY WITH RECEIVING NATION
MILGROUP POC PRIOR TO PROCESSING REQUISITIONS/SHIPMENTS)
- 7.62MM AMMO LINKED FOR 1,000,000    $    650,000
   USE WITH GAU-17 MINIGUN
   DODAC 1305-A165
(COLAR, COLNAV, FAC ALLOCATIONS TBD)
(AIR FORCE WILL COORDINATE AMMUNITION DODAC REQUIREMENTS/AVAILABILITY WITH RECEIVING NATION
MILGROUP POC PRIOR TO PROCESSING REQUISITIONS/SHIPMENTS)
- FUEL                                 $2,500,000
  (SEE DETAILED INSTRUCTIONS ON PARAGRAPH 10)
- RUNWAY CRATERING      50          $     35,000
  CHARGES
  (COLAR 100%)
- FLIGHT EQUIPMENT
  NOT TO EXCEED                     $    550,000
   (COLAR, COLNAV, FAC ALLOCATIONS TBD)
  -- HELMETS
  -- FLIGHT SUITS
  -- GLOVES
  -- SURVIVAL GEAR
  -- FLAK VESTS
  -- 9MM PISTOL HOLSTERS
  -- FLARE PISTOLS
  -- FLASHLIGHTS
  -- OXYGEN MASKS
- MOBILE TRAINING TEAM
  -- TEAMS FOR EMERGENCY
     MEDICINE TRAINING  3          $    100,000
  -- C-130 AIRCRAFT
     MAINTENANCE TRAINING          $    100,000
TOTAL DRAWDOWN AUTHORITY PROVIDED BY THE DEPARTMENT OF THE AIR FORCE FOR THE COLOMBIAN MILITARY
BY
THIS EXECUTE ORDER NOT TO EXCEED       $14,152,500


DEPARTMENT OF THE AIR FORCE IS AUTHORIZED TO PROVIDE USMILGROUP COLOMBIA, UNDER SECTION 506(A)(2)
AUTHORITY, THE FOLLOWING SERVICE.  REQUEST DELIVERY OF THE FOLLOWING SERVICE TO USMILGROUP
COLOMBIA:

ITEM                              VALUE
LOGISTICIAN (TDY) TO SUPPORT
OPERATIONS AT USMILGROUP
COLOMBIA                          $60,000
NOTES:  TDY NOT TO EXCEED 180 DAYS.  USMILGROUP COLOMBIA WILL COORDINATE DETAILS OF TDY DATES AND
CALL-UP MESSAGE REQUIREMENTS WITH THE AIR FORCE.
TOTAL DRAWDOWN AUTHORITY PROVIDED BY THE DEPARTMENT OF THE AIR FORCE FOR USMILGROUP COLOMBIA BY
THIS EXECUTE ORDER NOT TO EXCEED       $60,000


DEPARTMENT OF THE AIR FORCE IS AUTHORIZED TO PROVIDE THE PERUVIAN MILITARY, UNDER SECTION
506(A)(2) AUTHORITY, THE FOLLOWING STOCKS, SERVICES AND/OR TRAINING.  REQUEST DELIVERY OF THE
FOLLOWING INVENTORY AND RESOURCES TO THE PERUVIAN MILITARY:

ITEM              QUANTITY          VALUE
- A-37 SPARE PARTS  VARIOUS         $1,800,000
   (PERU AIR FORCE)
TOTAL DRAWDOWN AUTHORITY PROVIDED BY THE DEPARTMENT OF THE AIR FORCE FOR THE PERUVIAN MILITARY BY
THIS EXECUTE ORDER NOT TO EXCEED       $1,800,000


DEPARTMENT OF THE AIR FORCE IS AUTHORIZED TO PROVIDE THE ECUADORIAN MILITARY, UNDER SECTION
506(A)(2) AUTHORITY, THE FOLLOWING STOCKS, SERVICES AND/OR TRAINING. REQUEST DELIVERY OF THE
FOLLOWING INVENTORY AND RESOURCES TO THE ECUADORIAN MILITARY:

ITEM              QUANTITY          VALUE
- C-130 SPARE PARTS                $1,850,000
   (ECUADOR AIR FORCE)
```

TOTAL DRAWDOWN AUTHORITY PROVIDED BY THE DEPARTMENT OF THE AIR FORCE FOR THE ECUADORIAN MILITARY BY
THIS EXECUTE ORDER NOT TO EXCEED $1,850,000

DEPARTMENT OF THE AIR FORCE IS AUTHORIZED TO PROVIDE THE PANAMANIAN NATIONAL POLICE, UNDER
SECTION 506(A)(2) AUTHORITY, THE FOLLOWING STOCKS, SERVICES AND/OR TRAINING. REQUEST DELIVERY OF
THE FOLLOWING INVENTORY AND RESOURCES TO THE PANAMANIAN NATIONAL POLICE:

ITEM	QUANTITY	VALUE
- POLICE SUPPORT EQUIPMENT NOT TO EXCEED		$ 10,000
- VEHICLES (VANS 8-10 PASSENGER)	2	$ 40,000

TOTAL DRAWDOWN AUTHORITY PROVIDED BY THE DEPARTMENT OF THE AIR FORCE FOR THE PANAMANIAN NATIONAL
POLICE BY
THIS EXECUTE ORDER NOT TO EXCEED $ 50,000

TOTAL TRANSPORTATION DRAWDOWN AUTHORITY FOR AIR FORCE PROVIDED FOR
THIS PD IS: $2,148,667

TOTAL DRAWDOWN AUTHORITY PROVIDED BY THE DEPARTMENT OF THE AIR FORCE THIS EXECUTE ORDER NOT TO
EXCEED $23,208,667
XXXXXXXXXXXXXXXXXXXXXXXXXXXXXXXXXXXXXXXXXXXXXXXXXXXXXXXXXXXXXX
TOTAL DRAWDOWN AUTHORITY FOR DOD PORTION
OF PD99-43 $69,700,000
TOTAL DRAWDOWN AUTHORITY FOR THIS
EXECUTE ORDER. $69,626,000
TOTAL REMAINING DRAWDOWN AUTHORITY
FOR DOD UNDER PD99-43 $ 74,000
XXXXXXXXXXXXXXXXXXXXXXXXXXXXXXXXXXXXXXXXXXXXXXXXXXXXXXXXXXXXXX

> DRAWDOWNS **DO NOT** PROVIDE OBLIGATION-AL AUTHORITY USE **DRAW-DOWN AUTHORITY** THROUGHOUT THE EXORD SEE C1 2 4

10. FUEL. AS COORDINATED WITH SOUTHCOM, DLA (DESC), JOINT STAFF J4, MAAG LIMA PERU, AND
BOGOTA COLOMBIA, FUEL WILL BE PROVIDED BY THE DEFENSE ENERGY SUPPORT CENTER FROM DESC BULK FUEL
TERMINALS(CONUS/OCONUS) VIA CONTRACT/ORGANIC CARRIER TO DESIGNATED PORTS IN PERU AND COLOMBIA.
THE SERVICES ARE TASKED TO PROVIDE THE AMOUNTS SHOWN BELOW VIA MILITARY INTER-DEPARTMENTAL
PURCHASE REQUEST (MIPR) TO DESC. EACH INVOLVED MILDEP MUST FORWARD ONE MIPR CITING ONLY ONE O&M
APPROPRIATION WITH A COMPLETE LINE OF ACCOUNTING TO INCLUDE A VALID BILLABLE DODAAC AND A
COMPLETE BILLING MAILING ADDRESS BY AT LEAST TWO WEEKS (DATES TBD) BEFORE DESC LIFTS FUEL TO:

MS JEAN BLACKBURN, BUDGET OFFICER
DEFENSE ENERGY SUPPORT CENTER
8725 JOHN KINGMAN RD
SUITE 3934, ATTN DESC-RB
FORT BELVOIR, VA 22060-6621

SERVICES WILL STATE ON FACE OF MIPR, 'FUNDS ARE PROVIDED TO SUPPORT PRESIDENTIAL DETERMINATION
(PD) 99-43.' NO FURTHER DELINEATION WILL BE STATED. SERVICES MUST COORDINATE DETAILS OF THESE
TRANSACTIONS WITH DESC POC MR. RICHARD SNINSKY, ASSISTANT TO COMPTROLLER, DEFENSE ENERGY SUPPORT
CENTER, AT DSN 427-8455, COMMERCIAL (703) 767-8455, EMAIL RSNINSKY@DESC.DLA.MIL. DD1155S AND
DD250S WILL BE IMMEDIATELY FAXED TO MS. CAROL RICHEY, DESC, FAX DSN 427-9380, FAX COMMERCIAL
(703)767-9380.
A. NAVY: $ 10,500,000 IN O&M FUNDS FOR USE BY DESC TO PAY FOR REORDER OF FUEL DRAWDOWN AS TASKED
UNDER PD 99-43.
B. AIR FORCE: $ 3,500,000 IN O&M FUNDS FOR USE BY DESC TO PAY FOR REORDER OF FUEL DRAWDOWN AS
TASKED UNDER PD 99-43.
C. NAVY, AIR FORCE: $1,000,000 EACH IN O&M FUNDS FOR USE BY DLA-DESC FOR TRANSPORT (FOR TOTAL
OF $2,000,000). FUNDS WILL COME OUT OF TRANSPORTATION LINE AUTHORIZED TO EACH MILDEP ON THIS
EXECUTE ORDER. UNUSED TRANSPORTATION FUNDS WILL REVERT BACK TO SERVICES ONCE FUEL TRANSFERS ARE
COMPLETED.
D. DLA: COORDINATE WITH SERVICES, SOUTHCOM AND COUNTRY TEAMS THE PURCHASE, TRANSPORT
($2,000,000 VALUE) AND DELIVERY OF ALL FUEL TO COLOMBIA ($13,000,000 FUEL VALUE) AND PERU
($1,000,000 FUEL VALUE).
E. COUNTRY TEAMS ARE RESPONSIBLE FOR DETERMINING THE ALLOCATION OF FUEL IN ACCORDANCE WITH THE
COUNTRIES COUNTERNARCOTICS OPERATIONAL REQUIREMENTS.
11. THE OVERALL POINT OF CONTACT FOR THIS DRAWDOWN IS MR. JOHN GERLAUGH, DSCA/ERASA/ASA, DSN
329-3722, COMMERCIAL {703} 601-3722, FACSIMILE (703)604-6547, E-MAIL (UNCLAS)
GERLAUGHJ@OSD.PENTAGON.MIL, POC FOR REPORTING PROGRAMMED AND/OR DELIVERED COMMODITIES AND
SERVICES ALONG WITH THEIR ASSOCIATED COSTS IN THE DSCA 1000 SYSTEM IS MS. HELEN MOORE,
DSCA/COMPT-FM, DSN 329-3740 OR COMMERCIAL {703}601-3740; MILDEP POCS ARE: ARMY IS MS. VALERIE
MCCAULEY, DSN 425-8084COMMERCIAL (703)588-8084; NAVY IS COMMANDER WILLIAM MCISSAC, DSN 764-2657,
COMMERCIAL (202) 764-2690; AIR FORCE IS MR. GLENN KELLER, DSN 425-8871, COMMERCIAL (703) 588-
8871; JOINT STAFF IS LT COL NACTION OFFICERMI MANADIER, J4/SILD DSN 227-6492, COMMERCIAL (703)

697-6492; DLA IS LINDA KIMBERLIN, DSN 427-7515, COMMERCIAL (703) 767-7515. MILDEP 1000 SYSTEM POCS ARE: ARMY, SAM RHOADS, AMSAC-IM, NEW CUMBERLAND PA, DSN 977-6679, COMM 717-770-6679; NAVY, DAVE MOLYNEAUX, NAVICP, PHILADELPHIA PA, DSN 442-4473, COML 215-697-4473; AIR FORCE, B.J. LIGHTNER, AFSAC-IPS, DSN 787-1132 EXT. 4173, COML 932-257-1132.

TERMINATION MESSAGE

R 141907Z NOV 03
FM SECDEF WASHINGTON DC//DSCA-IT// TO ZEN/OSDNTS UC
INFO DMSCHAIRS TEST AMHS
BT
UNCLAS
SUBJECT: TERMINATION OF SECTION 506 (A) (1) DRAWDOWN IN SUPPORT OF UNITED N IONS
MISSION IN SIERRA LEONE (UNAMSIL). FINAL CLOSURE ACTION OTHERORG
UNCLASSIFIED//
UNCLASSIFIED//
UNCLASSIFIED// UNCLAS
==============================PASS TO INSTRUCTIONS:
HQDA CSA PASS TO SAAL AND [Copy TO] SAAL-NI
NAVY IPO PASS TO 260 AND 280
CDRUSASAC PASS TO AMSAC-MM NAVICP PASS TO 755C
AFSAC PASS TO CO AND GB AND IA AND SD AND FM DLA PASS TO ESOC AND DLSC-CI AND DLSC-CP

PAGE 02 RUEWDAS8887 UNCLAS JOINT STAFF PASS TO J8
HQ USEUCOM PASS TO ECCM CDRSDDC PASS TO MTOP-OS DFAS PASS TO OFC-SYM
SECSTATE PASS TO PM AND AF
SUBJECT: TERMINATION OF SECTION 506 (A) (1) DRAWDOWN IN SUPPORT OF UNITED NATIONS
MISSION IN SIERRA LEONE (UNAMSIL). FINAL CLOSURE ACTION REFS:
A. PRESIDENTIAL DETERMINATION (PD) 00-27, SIGNED 21 JULY 2000
B. SECDEF, DSCA, MSG 152123Z AUG 00, SUBJECT: FYOO 506(A) (1) DRAWDOWN IN SUPPORT OF
    UNITED NATIONS MISSION IN SIERRA LEONE (UNAMSIL), GENERAL INSTRUCTIONS AND EXECUTE
    ORDER ONE.
C. SECDEF, DSCA, MSG 171841Z AUG 00, SUBJECT: FYOO 506(A) (1) DRAWDOWN IN SUPPORT OF
    UNITED NATIONS MISSION IN SIERRA LEONE (UNAMSIL), GENERAL INSTRUCTIONS AND EXECUTE
    ORDER TWO.
D. SECDEF, DSCA, MSG 061240Z SEP 00, SUBJECT: FYOO 506(A) (1)
PAGE 03 RUEWDAS8887 UNCLAS
    DRAWDOWN IN SUPPORT OF UNITED NATIONS MISSION IN SIERRA LEONE (UNAMSIL), GENERAL
    INSTRUCTIONS AND EXECUTE ORDER THREE.
E. SECDEF, DSCA, MSG 281102Z SEP 00, SUBJECT: FYOO 506(A) (1) DRAWDOWN IN SUPPORT OF
    UNITED NATIONS MISSION IN SIERRA LEONE (UNAMSIL), GENERAL INSTRUCTIONS AND EXECUTE
    ORDER FOUR.
F. SECDEF, DSCA, MSG 2913SSZ SEP 00, SUBJECT: FYOO 506(A) (1)
    DRAWDOWN IN SUPPORT OF UNITED NATIONS MISSION IN SIERRA LEONE (UNAMSIL), EXECUTE
    ORDER FIVE.
G. SECDEF, DSCA, MSG 041614Z OCT 00, SUBJECT: FYOO 506(A) (1) DRAWDOWN IN SUPPORT OF
    UNITED NATIONS MISSION IN SIERRA LEONE (UNAMSIL), EXECUTE ORDER SIX.
H. SECDEF, DSCA, MSG 301303Z OCT 00, SUBJECT: FYOO 506(A) (1) DRAWDOWN IN SUPPORT OF
    UNITED NATIONS MISSION
    IN SIERRA LEONE (UNAMSIL), EXECUTE ORDER SEVEN.
I. SECDEF, DSCA, MSG 121326Z DEC 00, SUBJECT: FYOO 506(A) (1) DRAWDOWN IN SUPPORT OF
    UNITED NATIONS MISSION IN SIERRA LEONE (UNAMSIL), EXECUTE ORDER EIGHT.
PAGE 04 RUEWDAS8887 UNCLAS
1. THIS MESSAGE TERMINATES THE DRAWDOWN AUTHORITY FOR ANY ADDITIONAL EQUIPMENT OR SERVICES
ASSOCIATED WITH THE AUTHORITY IN REFERENCES A THROUGH I ABOVE.
2. EFFECTIVE IMMEDIATELY, NO FURTHER ACTION WILL BE TAKEN TO DRAW DOWN DEPARTMENT OF
DEFENSE EQUIPMENT, SERVICES, OR TRAINING UNDER THE AUTHORITIES OF PD 00-27.
3. SERVICES WILL REPORT FINAL ACTIVITIES PER INSTRUCTIONS IN REFS A THROUGH I,
INCLUDING FINAL COSTS ASSOCIATED WITH THE SUBJECT DRAW DOWN INTO THE DSCA-1000 SYSTEM
IAW REFERENCES A THROUGH K WITHIN 60 DAYS OF RECEIPT OF THIS MESSAGE.
4. POINTS OF CONTACT: MS. DONNA GALADA, DSCA, (703) 604-6639. MS. MARGE WEBB,
DSCA/COMPT, (703) 601-3741. MR. MICHAEL EVANS, DSCA/COMPT, (703) 604-6613. QUESTIONS
REGARDING RECONCILIATION SHOULD BE DIRECTED TO MR. JOSEPH RACHAL AT (703) 604-6600.
DSN FOR 601 PREFIX IS 329, AND DSN 664 FOR PREFIX 604.

MILDEP
AO
Actions
required

CONGRESSIONAL LETTER

In reply refer to:
I-00/14393-FM

The Honorable Jerry Lewis
Chairman, Committee on Appropriations
House of Representatives
Washington, DC 20515

Dear Mr. Chairman:

This report is made pursuant to the requirements of Section 506(b)(2) of the Foreign Assistance Act of 1961, as amended, to inform you that the Department of Defense completed delivery of the defense articles and services on the attached list by December 1997.

Pursuant to Section 506(a)(1) of the Act, Presidential Determination 96-55 (PD), dated 30 September 1996, directed the provision of defense articles from the stocks of the Department of Defense, defense services of the Department of Defense, and military education and training to provide assistance to the countries that participated in the Economic Community of West African States' Peacekeeping Force (ECOMOG), to enhance ECOMOG's peacekeeping capabilities to bring about a peaceful solution to the crisis in Liberia. The PD authorized the drawdown of goods and services up to a total of $5,000,000.

Sincerely,

Attachment
As stated

ECONOMIC COMMUNITY OF WEST AFRICAN STATES'
PEACEKEEPING FORCE (ECOMOG)
Presidential Determination 96-55

The following countries received goods and services under Presidential Determination Number 96-55: Nigeria, Ghana, Sierra Leone, Mali and Guinea.

Cost Breakout of Goods and Services Provided to Participating Countries

($ in Thousands)

Organizational Clothing and Individual Equipment	332
Medical Supplies	1,349
Transportation	1,990
TOTAL	3,672

Prepared by: Margaret Webb, DSCA/COMPT/FM/IM, 703-601-3741, X37, PD96-55

Same letter to:	Distribution:
LEWIS, Chairman, HAC	ISA IA
KOLBE, Chairman, HACFO	OSD LA
HASTERT, Speaker of the House	STATE-PM-RSAT
CHENEY, President of the Senate	DSCA CHRON
STEVENS, (Sen) Chairman, SAC	DSCA ERASA-ASA
MCCONNELL, (Sen) Chairman, SACFO	DSCA LPP
HELMS, (Sen) Chairman, SFRC	

Copy of Chairman Lewis's letter to: LOWEY, Nita, HACFO (Attn: Beth Tritter, Rm 2421)

APPENDIX 7

For drawdown points of contact please refer to:
JOSEPH.RACHAL.CTR@DSCA.MIL

APPENDIX 8

AP8. APPENDIX 8

Example DSCA 1000 System Reporting

1000 ACCESS SYSTEM

To access the system, users must be able to access DSCA's Unclassified Network and have Access 2000 installed on their computer. A shortcut icon will be placed on their desktops to access the system. Users will double click on the icon and the system's Main Menu will appear as shown below.

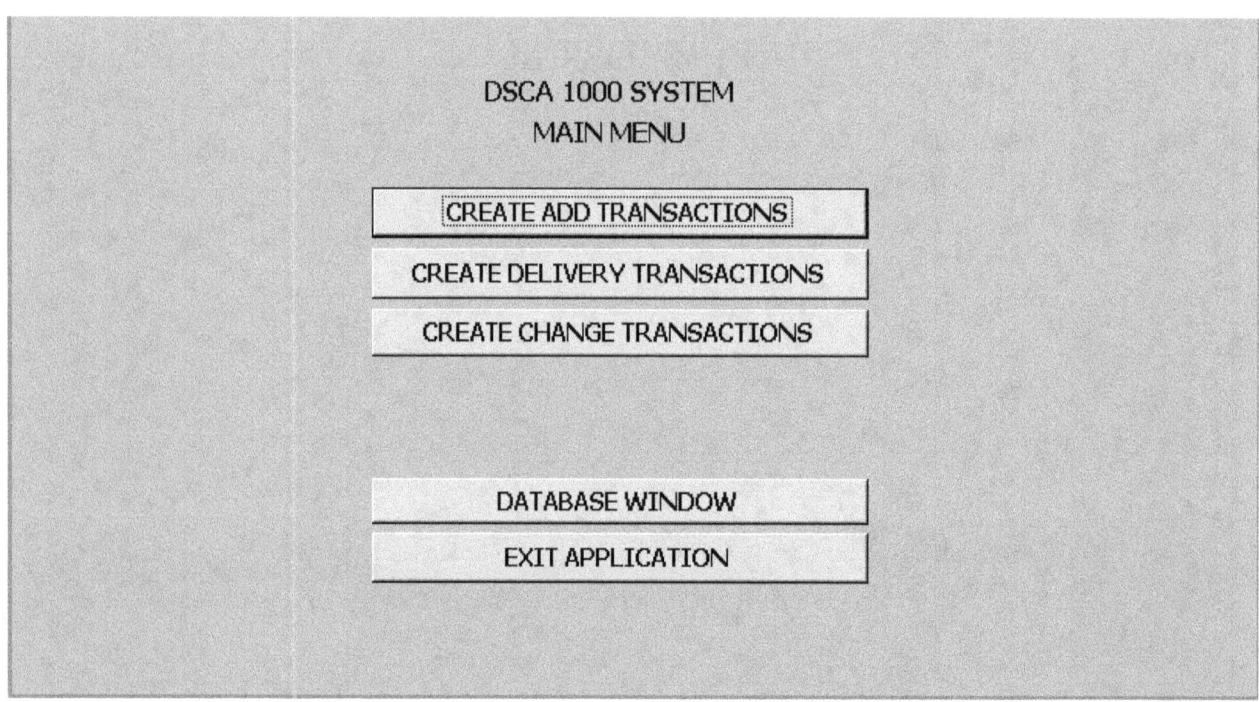

There are three options on this screen. Users will be able to create add, change and delivery transactions for the 1000 System update hosted on the Unclassified RISC6000 and create queries and reports from the Database Window option using the 1000 Master File.

The 1000 System Master File will be copied to this application after every update has been performed.

If you experience any problems with the 1000 Access System, please call Sandra Pinder at 703-601-3759.

CREATE MATERIEL ADD TRANSACTIONS

Click on the **CREATE ADD TRANSACTIONS** button and the following screen will appear.

```
                        1000 SYSTEM
              ADD TRANSACTION FOR MATERIEL  (3 CARD)


  * TRANSACTION CODE  [3 ]                          LEAD TIME  [ ]
  * RECORD CONTROL NUMBER  [    ]                  SPARE PARTS  [ ]
  * NATIONAL STOCK NUMBER  [         ]  COMMUNICATIONS/ANCILLARY CODE  [ ]
       * GENERIC CODE  [ ]                 * IMPLEMENTING AGENCY  [ ]
      COMMITMENT CODE  [ ]                            * STATUS  [F]
        * REASON CODE  [P3  ]                  FUNDING PRIORITY  [ ]
           QUANTITY  [ 00000]                    ISSUE PRIORITY  [ ]
  * PROGRAM ORIGINATOR CODE  [ ]              REQUIRED DELIVERY  [ ]
        * COUNTRY CODE  [  ]                  * SOURCE OF SUPPLY  [ ]
       CUSTOMER CODE  [  ]         * MILSTRIP ROUTING IDENTIFIER (MRI) CODE  [ ]
  SPECIAL SUPPLY PROCEDURE  [ ]          * CHANGE ORIGINATOR CODE  [ ]
  * TYPE OF ASSISTANCE CODE  [C]          SYSTEM IDENTIFIER CODE  [ ]
          UNIT PRICE  [        ]                  * FISCAL CODE  [ ]
        * PROGRAM YEAR  [  ]                               CRA  [ ]
      * MAP ELEMENT CODE  [   ]                      TOTAL COST  [00000000]


        [ADD A RECORD]   [WRITE MATERIEL      [RETURN TO 1000
                          TRANSACTIONS         SYSTEM MAIN MENU]
                          TO NETWORK]
```

The Transaction Code, Reason Code, Type of Assistance Code and Status fields have default values and can be changed.

The Quantity and Total Cost fields have default values of zeros. When entering a value in these fields make sure the value contain leading zeros.

Required fields for add transactions have an asterisk before the field name. If no data is entered or invalid data is entered, an error message will appear. After you have finished entering data on the screen, click on the **ADD A RECORD** button, to add the record to the MATERIEL table.

When you have finished adding all your transactions, click on the **WRITE MATERIEL TRANSACTIONS TO NETWORK** button. A file will be created on the network server for retrieval by the 1000 System Project Officer to update the 1000 System. An email message will be sent to the Project Officer that a file has been created for retrieval.

CREATE MATERIEL CHANGE TRANSACTIONS

Click on the **CREATE CHANGE TRANSACTIONS** button from the main menu and the following screen will appear.

```
                              1000 SYSTEM
                   CHANGE TRANSACTION FOR MATERIEL  (P TRANSACTION)


    * TRANSACTION CODE  [E  ]                          LEAD TIME  [  ]
  * RECORD CONTROL NUMBER [   ]                       SPARE PARTS  [  ]
  * NATIONAL STOCK NUMBER [        ]     COMMUNICATIONS/ANCILLARY CODE  [  ]
      * GENERIC CODE  [ ]                     * IMPLEMENTING AGENCY  [  ]
     COMMITMENT CODE  [ ]                                 * STATUS  [F ]
       * REASON CODE  [P3 ]                        FUNDING PRIORITY  [  ]
          QUANTITY  [00000]                          ISSUE PRIORITY  [  ]
 * PROGRAM ORIGINATOR CODE  [ ]                    REQUIRED DELIVERY  [  ]
      * COUNTRY CODE  [ ]                          * SOURCE OF SUPPLY  [  ]
      CUSTOMER CODE  [ ]          * MILSTRIP ROUTING IDENTIFIER (MRI) CODE  [  ]
 SPECIAL SUPPLY PROCEDURE  [ ]               * CHANGE ORIGINATOR CODE  [  ]
 * TYPE OF ASSISTANCE CODE  [C ]             SYSTEM IDENTIFIER CODE  [  ]
          UNIT PRICE  [       ]                       * FISCAL CODE  [  ]
      * PROGRAM YEAR  [   ]                                   CRA  [  ]
    * MAP ELEMENT CODE  [    ]                         TOTAL COST  [00000000]


         [ADD A          [WRITE MATERIEL      [RETURN TO 1000
          RECORD]         TRANSACTIONS         SYSTEM MAIN MENU]
                          TO NETWORK]
```

The Transaction Code, Reason Code, Type of Assistance Code and Status fields have default values and can be changed.

The Quantity and Total Cost fields have default values of zeros. When entering a value in these fields make sure the value contain leading zeros.

Required fields for change transactions have an asterisk before the field name. If no data is entered or invalid data is entered in these fields, an error message will appear. After you have finished entering data on the screen, click on the **ADD A RECORD** button, to add the record to the MATERIEL table.

When you have finished adding all your transactions, click on the **WRITE MATERIEL TRANSACTIONS TO NETWORK** button. A file will be created on the network server for retrieval by the 1000 System Project Officer to update the 1000 System. An email message will be sent to the Project Officer that a file has been created for retrieval.

CREATE DELIVERY TRANSACTIONS

Click on the **CREATE DELIVERY TRANSACTIONS** button and the following screen will appear.

1000 SYSTEM
DELIVERY TRANSACTION (8 CARD)

TRANSACTION CODE	[8]
RECORD CONTROL NUMBER	[ ]
COUNTRY CODE	[ ]
PROGRAM YEAR OF DRAWDOWN	[ ]
DELIVERY PERIOD	[ ]
CHANGE ORIGINATOR CODE	[ ]
TOTAL DELIVERY VALUE	[ ]

ADD A RECORD	WRITE DELIVERY TRANSACTIONS TO NETWORK	RETURN TO 1000 SYSTEM MAIN MENU

The Transaction Code field has a default value of **8**.

All fields on the Delivery Transaction screen are required. The Delivery Period field is the last two digits of the Fiscal Year and the current quarter. (Example: 032 are for Fiscal Year 2003, Quarter 2).

Make sure that the Total Delivery Value field has leading zeros entered before the value.

After you have finished entering data on the screen, click on the **ADD A RECORD** button, to add the record to the Delivery table.

When you have finished adding all your transactions, click on the **WRITE DELIVERY TRANSACTIONS TO NETWORK** button. A file will be created on the network for retrieval by the 1000 System Project Officer to update the 1000 System. An email message will be sent to the Project Officer that a file has been created for retrieval.

DSCA 1000 SYSTEM REPORT
U N C L A S S I F I E D

DSCA - DRAWDOWNS
DETAILED LISTING

COUNTRY CODE	IMPLEMENTING AGENCY	RCN	PROGRAM YEAR	DESCRIPTION	UNIFIED COMMAND	PD AUTHORIZED VALUE	APPROVED /FUNDED VALUE	TOTAL DELIVERED VALUE	UNDELIVERED VALUE
PD 0005									
IQ	B	BB89	02	DRAWDOWN SUPPLIES/SERVICES	L		500,000	204,800	295,200
IQ	B	BB90	02	DRAWDOWN SUPPLIES/SERVICES	L		500,000	48,562	451,438
				Total Mildep Value			1,000,000		
				Total Mildep Delivered Value				253,362	
				Total Mildep Undelivered Value					451,438
IQ	D	AC75	00	SEC 506(A) INSTRUCTION	L		3,470	3,470	0
IQ	D	AC01	00	SEC 506(A) INSTRUCTION	L		1,693	1,693	0
IQ	D	AC04	00	SEC 506(A) INSTRUCTION	L		19,629	19,629	0
IQ	D	AC70	00	SEC 506(A) INSTRUCTION	L		20,526	20,526	0
IQ	D	AC07	00	SEC 506(A) INSTRUCTION	L		16,821	16,821	0
IQ	D	AC10	00	SEC 506(A) INSTRUCTION	L		5,953	5,953	0
IQ	D	AC14	00	SEC 506(A) INSTRUCTION	L		393	393	0
IQ	D	AC15	00	TRANSPORTATION COSTS	L		36	36	0
IQ	D	AC16	00	SEC 506(A) INSTRUCTION	L		5,330	5,330	0
IQ	D	AC19	00	SEC 506(A) INSTRUCTION	L		19,269	19,269	0
IQ	D	AC22	00	SEC 506(A) INSTRUCTION	L		2,910	2,910	0
IQ	D	AC00	00	SEC 506(A) INSTRUCTION	L		13,849	13,849	0
IQ	D	AC28	00	SEC 506(A) INSTRUCTION	L		3,367	3,367	0
IQ	D	AC32	00	SEC 506(A) INSTRUCTION	L		2,731	2,731	0

Unified Command Codes: C = USACOM, E = EUCOM, L = CENTCOM, N = NONREGIONAL, P = PACOM, R = NORTHCOM, S = SOUTHCOM
Implementing Agency Codes: B = Army, D = Air Force and P = Navy

Wednesday, February 25, 2004

APPENDIX 8

DSCA 1000 SYSTEM REPORT

U N C L A S S I F I E D
DSCA - DRAWDOWNS
DETAILED LISTING

COUNTRY CODE	IMPLEMENTING AGENCY	RCN	PROGRAM YEAR	DESCRIPTION	UNIFIED COMMAND	PD AUTHORIZED VALUE	APPROVED /FUNDED VALUE	TOTAL DELIVERED VALUE	UNDELIVERED VALUE
PD 0005									
IQ	D	AC36	00	SEC 506(A) INSTRUCTION	L		2,883	2,883	0
IQ	D	AC40	00	SEC 506(A) INSTRUCTION	L		5,398	5,398	0
IQ	D	AC55	00	SEC 506(A) INSTRUCTION	L		8,432	8,432	0
IQ	D	AC80	00	SEC 506(A) INSTRUCTION	L		3,677	3,677	0
IQ	D	AC25	00	SEC 506(A) INSTRUCTION	L		2,856	2,856	0
				Total Mildep Value			139,223		
				Total Mildep Delivered Value				139,223	
				Total Mildep Undelivered Value					0
				Total PD Value:			1,139,223		
				Total PD Delivered Value:				392,585	
				Total PD Undelivered Value:					0

Unified Command Codes: C = USACOM, E = EUCOM, L = CENTCOM, N = NONREGIONAL, P = PACOM, R = NORTHCOM, S = SOUTHCOM
Implementing Agency Codes: B = Army, D = Air Force and P = Navy

Wednesday, February 25, 2004

APPENDIX 8

APPENDIX 9

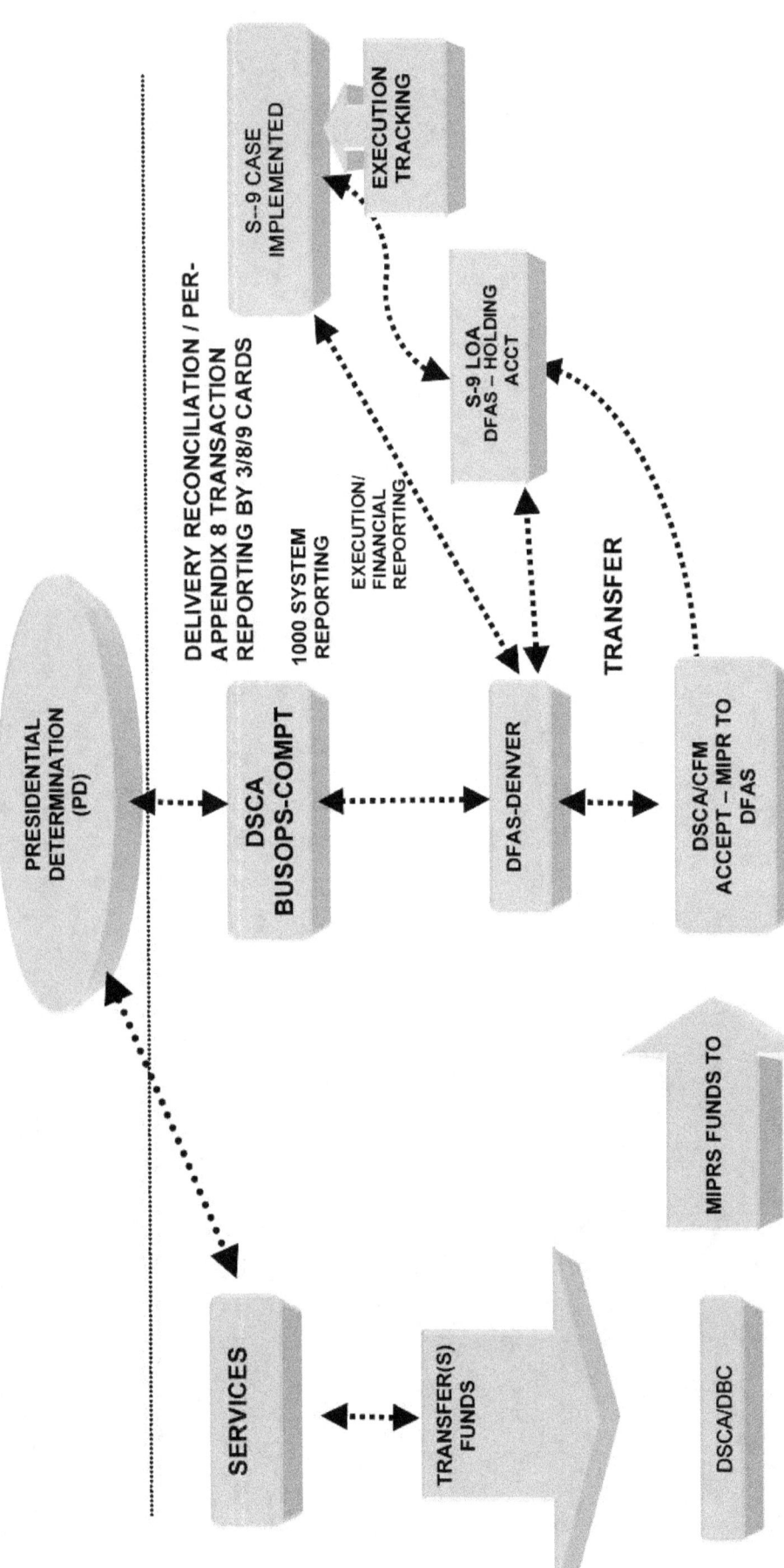

AP9. APPENDIX 9

PRESIDENTIAL DETERMINED DRAWDOWN: FLOW OF FUNDS

DELIVERY RECONCILIATION / PER-
APPENDIX 8 TRANSACTION
REPORTING BY 3/8/9 CARDS

1000 SYSTEM
REPORTING

EXECUTION/
FINANCIAL
REPORTING

PRESIDENTIAL
DETERMINATION
(PD)

DSCA
BUSOPS-COMPT

DFAS-DENVER

DSCA/CFM
ACCEPT – MIPR TO
DFAS

S-9 CASE
IMPLEMENTED

EXECUTION
TRACKING

S-9 LOA
DFAS – HOLDING
ACCT

TRANSFER

SERVICES

TRANSFER(S)
FUNDS

MIPRS FUNDS TO

DSCA/DBC

Note: The FLOW of Funds: DSCA promulgate the PD to the Services
- The Services transfers the funds to DSCA/DBC
- DSCA/DBC MIPRs the funds to DSCA/CFM
- DSCA/CFM accepts the MIPR and then transmits the MIPR to DFAS-Denver
- DFAS-Denver draws the funds into an S9 holding account for that drawdown
- When the S9 case is implemented, DFAS-Denver places the funds in the LOA
- DFAS-Denver reports the expenditures of funds to DSCA BUSOPS-COMPT

INDEX

INDEX